To Margaret
HAPPY CHRISTM
love from &

GW00995247

God's Little Errand Boys

Christian clergymen who helped
the Jews come home

YANKY FACHLER

Copyright © Yanky Fachler, 2011
The author has asserted his moral rights.

ISBN: 978-1-908417-19-0

Published in 2011 by The History Publisher
an imprint of The Universal Publishing Group

www.theuniversalpublishinggroup.com

A CIP Catalogue record for this book is available from
The British Library and the Irish Copyright Libraries.

All rights reserved. No part of this publication may be copied, reproduced or transmitted
in any form or by any means, without the prior permission of the publishers.
The rights for images used remain with the originator.

Designed, typeset, printed and bound in Ireland by The Book Producers Ltd.

www.thebookproducers.ie

Contents

Also by Yanky Fachler:

6 Officers, 2 Lions and 750 Mules
The Vow: Rebuilding the Fachler tribe after the Holocaust
Fire in the Belly
Chutzpah
The Bookbuzz book of business insights 2009
The Bookbuzz book of business insights 2011
The Bookbuzz book of business execution
Selling Conversations (with Dermot McConkey)

Introduction

The story of the *Exodus* (the ship that tried to break Britain's blockade of Palestine in 1947, not the flight of the Israelites from Egypt 3,500 years earlier), as immortalized by Leon Uris, has inspired millions.

I was recently reminiscing with Professor David Alexander. Alex and I both attended Carmel College, a Jewish boarding school in England, in the late 50s. Out of the blue, Alex said: "You cannot imagine what a huge impact *Exodus* had on me as a 13-year-old."

I did a double take. Alex had repeated my oft-repeated sentiments, word for word.

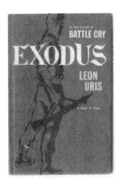

Screenwriter and reporter Uris was hired by Edward Gottlieb, an American PR man seeking to improve Israel's image in the United States, to write a novel about Israel's origin. Uris built his story around the passengers aboard the *Exodus*.

When the book was published in the USA in 1958, it became an international publishing phenomenon, and was the biggest bestseller since *Gone with the Wind*.

When I read *Exodus,* I knew that I had found my identity. Not that I needed too much help in that direction. Both my parents were ardent Zionists, and we had almost moved to Israel when I was four.

But no one had ever laid out the historical context of the birth of the State of Israel the way in which Uris did in *Exodus*. And I was not alone. Dozens of my contemporaries had a similar experience. We read the book in high school, and the effect, even on those who did not especially like novels, was electric. *Exodus* triggered the decision of generations of readers to make aliya and go and live in Israel.

There is no doubt that as a novel, *Exodus* is flawed. The writing is sometimes sloppy. Uris took liberties with historical accuracy. He adopted a largely Labour Movement narrative at the expense of the Revisionist narrative.

But the effect of reading the book on me was seismic. *Exodus* made me much more aware of important historical facts: Dreyfus, pogroms, Holocaust, DP camps, Warsaw Ghetto, Declaration of Independence – themes that I would write and lecture on in later life.

I learned for the first time just how two-faced the British had been. As a loyal British subject, who idolized Winston Churchill, I was filled with revulsion. I remember going to my parents and demanding to know how they could possibly support a Labour Party that had included Ernest Bevin, Britain's anti-Zionist Foreign Secretary between WW2 and Israel's War of Independence.

I will be eternally grateful to Mr Uris for his book.

I had always been fascinated by the story of the rickety boat trying to reach pre-state Israel. But Uris either did not know about – or chose not to mention - one very special person on the boat.

The Reverend John Grauel, an American member of the Haganah, was the only Christian among thousands of Jews. He was on board for a mission that only a Christian could fulfill. He was there to ensure that the story of what happened on the *Exodus* reached the outside world – since a Jew's version of the story would carry less credibility.

The Grauel story led me to research other Christian clergymen who impacted on the story of the Jewish struggle for independence, and these Christians are the subject of this book.

This is my second time that I have written about Christians who helped the Zionist cause. In *The Vow*, which traces my parents' escape from Nazi Germany before WW2, I describe how in March 1944, my father Eli - then a 21-year-old German-born refugee with Polish nationality, joined the Royal Fusiliers. He unsuccessfully tried to be transferred to the Jewish Brigade, a unit about which I knew very little.

As soon as I finished *The Vow*, I started researching the role of the Jewish Brigade. I discovered that to understand the origins of this unit, I first had to learn about two earlier Jewish units in WW1: the Jewish Legion, and the Assyrian Jewish Refugee Mule Corps, also known as the Zion Mule Corps.

This led me to the man who commanded both units, Irish Protestant John Henry Patterson. In *6 Officers, 2 Lions and 750 Mules*, I explored how the infant Jewish state withstood the military onslaught of five invading Arab armies in May 1948. I identified six British army officers who, in the 25-year period 1915-1940, spearheaded the re-emergence of a Jewish military ethos after almost 2,000 years.

All six Zionist officers believed that Jews should organize themselves into a proactive military force. All six Zionist officers battled against what they regarded as institutionalized anti-Semitism in the British army.

The three Jewish officers were: Vladimir Ze'ev Jabotinsky, journalist and Zionist activist; Captain Joseph Trumpeldor, the hero of the Russo-Japanese War; and Eliezer Margolin, an Australian officer.

The three Christian officers were Patterson; Richard Meinertzhagen, an Intelligence Officer who served under General Allenby; and Orde Wingate, who created the Special Night Squads during the Arab Revolt.

Left to right: Patterson, Wingate, Meinertzhagen

Inspired by Grauel, I shifted my scope from Christians who influenced the military ethos, to Christians who influenced the political process that led to the very creation of the Jewish state.

They are the American Reverend William Blackstone (the self-styled "God's Little Errand Boy"); the British-German Reverend William Hechler; the American Reverend John Stanley Grauel; the Canadian Reverend William Lovell Hull; American water expert Elwood Mead; and American soil expert Walter Clay Lowdermilk.

My thanks to Rory Miller for permission to use his article *Bible and Soil: Walter Clay Lowdermilk, the Jordan Valley Project and the Palestine Debate.*

I am indebted to Lauren Elise Apter, who gave me permission to use her unpublished doctoral thesis: *Disorderly Decolonization: the White Paper of 1939 and the End of British Rule in Palestine.*

And I am especially indebted to my friend and colleague Jerry Klinger of the Jewish American Society for Historic Preservation, whose pointed me to Christians "who could do what no Jew could do."

In 2000, over 150 Jewish Orthodox and non-Orthodox scholars, teachers and rabbis signed *Dabru Emet* (Speak truth), a Jewish reassessment of Christians. The document calls on Jews to learn about the efforts of Christians to honour Judaism. I dedicate this book to the efforts of six Christians who honoured Judaism by helping Jews return to their ancient homeland.

CHAPTER 1

British, American and French Christians – and the Restoration of Jews in Palestine

When we talk about the Restoration of the Jews to their ancient homeland, it is often in a predominantly Christian context.

Strictly speaking, of course, Jews had been pining for their ancient Jewish homeland for two thousand years. It has been the focus of Jewish education, Jewish tradition and Jewish prayers since the fall of Jerusalem in the Jewish Revolt against the Romans in 70 CE. All Jewish ritual centres on a return to Israel.

Each year, Jews sit down for the most important meal in the Jewish calendar, the Seder meal on Passover. As they recall the liberation of the Israelite slaves from bondage in Egypt, they express the fervent wish:

"Next year in Jerusalem."

Christian theologians started openly discussing the notion that the Jews should return to Palestine in the sixteenth century. In 1589, Cambridge scholar Francis Kett was burned alive by the Church for his book, *The Glorious and Beautiful Garland of Man's Glorification Containing the Godly Misterie of Heavenly Jerusalem,* in which he mentioned "the notion of Jewish national return to Palestine."

In 1607, the Reverend Thomas Brightman wrote *Revelation of the Revelation* in which he asked, "What, shall they return to Jerusalem again? There is nothing more certain; the prophets do everywhere confirm it and beat upon it."

English Puritans Ebenezer and Joanna Cartwright petitioned the British Government in 1649 to assist Jews to move to Palestine: "That this Nation of England, with the inhabitants of the Netherlands, shall be the first and the readiest to transport Israel's sons and daughters on their ships to the land promised to their forefathers, Abraham, Isaac and Jacob for an everlasting inheritance."

Sir Isaac Newton was also a keen champion of the right of the Jews to return to their land. In 1733, he asserted that according to his scriptural interpretation of the Book of Daniel, the Jews would be assisted by another nation - Britain - to regain their ancient land.

In 1771, Joseph Eyre published *Observations Upon Prophecies Relating To The Restoration Of The Jews*, in which he refers to biblical prophecies concerning the descendants of Abraham, whom he believes should occupy the land known as Palestine.

In America, too, Christians were moved to write about the Restoration of the Jews. Reverend Ezra Stiles, Congregationalist minister, academic and educator, was a prominent supporter of restoration of the Jews. He learned Hebrew, and was able to translate large portions of the Hebrew Bible into English. As president of Yale between 1778 and 1795, Stiles also became its first professor of Semitics, and required all students to study Hebrew. He even delivered his first commencement address in Hebrew.

In 1783, Stiles wrote *The United States Elevated to Glory and Honour*, in which he writes: "There are three coetaneous events to take place whose fruition is certain from prophecy, the annihilation of the Pontificate, the reassembling of the Jews, and the fullness of the Gentiles."

British scientist Joseph Priestly wrote in 1799: "The land is uncultivated and ready to receive you, but the Turks control it. Their power must first fall. Therefore, I earnestly pray for its dissolution. But it may not happen for some time."

When Napoleon Bonaparte launched his campaign for the conquest of Palestine, he promised to restore the country to the Jews. On April 20 1799, he wrote: "Israelites, unique nation, whom, in thousands of years, lust of conquest and tyranny have been able to be deprived of their ancestral lands, but not of name and national existence!

"Arise then, with gladness, ye exiled! A war unexampled in the annals of history, waged in self-defence by a nation whose hereditary lands were regarded by its enemies as plunder to be divided, arbitrarily and at their convenience, by a stroke of the pen of Cabinets, avenges its own shame and the shame of the remotest nations, long forgotten under the yoke of slavery, and also, the almost two-thousand-year-old ignominy put upon you; and, while time and circumstances would seem to be least favourable to a restatement of your claims or even to their expression, and indeed to be compelling their complete abandonment, it offers to you at this very time, and contrary to all expectations, Israel's patrimony!

"Rightful heirs of Palestine! The great nation which does not trade in men and countries as did those which sold your ancestors unto all people (Joel, 3:6) herewith calls on you …. to remain master of it to maintain it against all comers.

"Hasten!, Now is the moment, which may not return for thousands of years, to claim the restoration of civic rights among the population of the universe which had been shamefully withheld from you for thousands of years, your political existence as a nation among the nations, and the unlimited natural right to worship Jehovah in accordance with your faith, publicly and most probably forever (Joel 4.20)."

Napoleon even reconvened the Sanhedrin, the body of 70 learned rabbis and scholars that had not met for almost 2,000 years.

The meeting of the Sanhedrin in 1807

Napoleon himself never saw his plans reach fruition. But his example seems to have inspired a distinguished gallery of 19th century clerics, writers, industrialists, artists and statesmen to write about the idea of Jewish restoration in Palestine.

11

In 1808, Presbyterian Asa McFarland predicted that the fall of the Ottoman Empire was imminent and that "the Jews will begin to be restored."

In 1809, a group of British evangelicals formed the London Jews' Society or the London Society for Promoting Christianity Among the Jews.

Although this was formed as an Anglican missionary society, one of its founding principles was to encourage the physical restoration of the Jewish people to the Land of Israel. The society has undergone several name changes. Church Missions to Jews, then The Church's Mission to the Jews, followed by The Church's Ministry Among the Jews, and finally to the current name of The Church's Ministry Among Jewish People (CMJ), which was adopted in 1995. Not all Anglicans are comfortable with the CMJ's original missionary focus. In 1992, George Carey became the first Archbishop of Canterbury in 150 years to decline to be Patron of CMJ, on the grounds that the organisation's missionary work damaged interfaith relations.

In the same year as the London Society was formed, 1809, Thomas Witherby wrote *The Restoration of the Jews - the Crisis of All Nations*. Like many British Christians, Witherby believed that Britain was destined to play a part in Israel's restoration.

Many Americans believed that it was America that was destined to play this role.

In 1825, US President John Quincy Adams wrote on behalf of the Jews: "I really wish the Jews again in Judea, an independent Nation..." He foresaw "a hundred thousand Israelites...well disciplined as the French army" that would march into Palestine and conquer it.

President Abraham Lincoln would say in 1863: "Restoring the Jews to their homeland is a noble dream shared by many Americans."

In 1838, in *Letters on Egypt, Edom and the Holy Land*, Lord Lindsay wrote:"The Jewish race, so wonderfully preserved, may yet have another stage of national existence opened to them, may once more obtain possession of their native land. The soil of Palestine...only waits for the return of her banished children, and the application of industry, commensurate with her agricultural capabilities, to burst once more into universal luxuriance."

In 1839, the Earl of Shaftesbury published an essay, *The State and Restoration of the Jews* in The Quarterly Review, in which he argued that "the Jews must be encouraged to return (to Palestine) in yet greater numbers and become once more the husbandman of Judea and Galilee."

13

Two Church of Scotland missionaries, Andrew Bonar and Robert Murray McCheyne, published a *Memorandum to the Protestant Monarchs of Europe* in 1839. The memorandum, which was printed verbatim by the London Times, called for the restoration of the Jews to Palestine.

In March 1841, a group of 320 Christian Memorialists sent a memorandum to the prime minister, Lord Palmerston: "Your Memorialists beg leave .... to remind your Lordship that the land of Palestine was bestowed by the Sovereign of the Universe upon the descendants of Abraham as a permanent and inalienable possession nearly 4000 years ago, and that neither conquests nor treaties among men can possibly affect their Title to it. He has also decreed that they shall again return to their country, and that the Gentiles shall be employed as a means of their restoration."

In 1844, Pastor T. Tully Crybace founded the British and Foreign Society for Promoting the Restoration of the Jewish Nation to Palestine. Also in 1844, a professor of Hebrew at New York University, George Bush, two of whose descendants would become President, published a tract entitled, *The Valley of the Vision, or The Dry Bones of Israel Revived.* He called for "elevating" the Jews "to a rank of honorable repute among the nations of the earth" by restoring them to the land of Israel.

Sir George Gawler, a former governor of South Australia, and founder of the Palestine Colonisation Fund, proposed a remedy for the desolation of the country: "Replenish the deserted towns and fields of Palestine with the energetic people whose warmest affections are rooted in the soil," he wrote in 1845.

In 1845, Edward Ledwich Mitford, a political ally of Palmerston, published "An appeal in Behalf of the Israel Nation in Connection with the British Policy in the Levant." The piece called for the "final establishment of the Jewish nation in Palestine as a protected state under the guardianship of Great Britain."

In the aftermath of 1878 Prusso-Turkish War, there were unfounded reports that at the negotiations at the Congress of Berlin, Britain was proposing to declare a protectorate over Syria and Palestine and that Palestine would be restored to the Jews. The very fact that such rumours existed shows that Jewish restoration was already part of the public agenda.

British industrialist, Edward Cazalet advocated a Restorationist approach, proposing that England should help Jews immigrate to Palestine in order to participate in large development projects. He even proposed a university devoted to Hebrew studies in Jerusalem. His vision came to pass 35 years after his death with the establishment of the Hebrew University in 1918.

15

In 1886, Dr H. Grattan Guinness, the Irish Protestant preacher, wrote *Light for the Last Days*: "There can be no question that those who live to see this year of 1917 will have reached one of the most important, perhaps the most momentous, of these terminal years of crisis." 1917 was the year that the Balfour Declaration was published and the year that Allenby liberated Jerusalem from the Turks.

In 1890, the American Protestant preacher Reverend De Witt Talmage, of the Brooklyn Tabernacle, published *Twenty-Five Sermons on the Holy Land*. The arrival in Palestine of Jews from Russia, he said, was "only a beginning of the fulfillment of Divine prophecy, when these people shall take possession of the Holy Land. All the fingers of Providence nowadays are pointing toward that resumption of Palestine by the Israelites."

In the next chapter, we will see how in 1891, a new name would emerge among Christian champions of a Jewish state in Palestine.

CHAPTER 2

The Blackstone Memorial

Born in Adams County, New York in 1841, William
Eugene Blackstone ran a successful real estate office
outside Chicago after the Civil War. A self-taught lay
evangelist and Bible teacher in the Methodist Episcopal
Church, he deliberately chose to abandon business and
devote himself entirely to missionary work.

Blackstone believed that God had never abandoned his
special relationship with the Jewish people. Without
the Jewish Restoration, there could be no return of
Jesus

While at a YMCA convention, Blackstone asked the
Reverend James Hall Brooke, one of the foremost
ministers of the time, to write a tract about the
Second Coming that he could pass out to train
passengers on his travels. Instead, Brooke suggested
that Blackstone write it himself and that he would
publish it – which is how Blackstone came to write
Jesus is Coming.

Published in 1878, the book was probably the most widely-read book on the Second Coming in the 19th century. It has since sold millions of copies, and has been translated into almost 50 languages – including Yiddish.

Blackstone regarded the Jews as "God's sun-dial," as the fulcrum of history. Although at first, Blackstone focused on the Restoration of the Jews as a prelude to their conversion to Christianity, he eventually absolved the Jews of the need to convert.

In 1888, he travelled to Palestine to study the Jewish colonisation efforts at first-hand. He stopped en route to attend the General Missionary Conference in London, a key premillennialist gathering.

He returned home from Palestine with a renewed vigour, inspired by Jeremiah's prophecy of the rebuilding of Jerusalem. He also returned with a new sense of urgency, due his growing concern about events in Russia, where the virulently anti-Semitic May Laws were once again being enforced.

Determined to act decisively, he started planning The Conference on the Past, Present and Future of Israel, which was held in 1890 in the First Methodist Episcopal Church in Chicago.

This conference is thought to be the first involving both Christians and Jews in America. Participants included Rabbi Dr. Emil G. Hirsch, who taught Judaism at the University of Chicago, and Dr. Bernhard Felsenthal, one of the founders of Chicago's pre-Herzl Zionist movement.

The conference passed the following unanimous resolution:

"The President of the United States is to be petitioned on the propriety of calling an International Conference to consider the condition of the Jews in modern nations and the possibility of opening a way for their restoration to Palestine."

Copies of the resolutions were forwarded to the Tsar as well as to other world leaders.

But Blackstone realized that conference resolutions would not ameliorate the condition of the persecuted Jews in Russia. In his self-proclaimed role as "God's Little Errand Boy", he recognized the disastrous consequences of Russia's death wish for its Jews.

Linking his desire for a solution to the suffering of the Jews of Russia, with his personal faith in the restoration of the Jews, he decided to enlist the help of the President of the United States.

Within four months of the conference, Blackstone had drafted the text of *Palestine for the Jews*, known to posterity as the Blackstone Memorial. Dated February 1891, the Memorial was signed by 413 governmental, business, and religious leaders from Chicago, Boston, New York, Philadelphia, Baltimore, and Washington, D.C.

This impressive list includes the Chief Justice of the United States Supreme Court, the Speaker of the House of Representatives, senators, congressmen, governors, Ohio Congressman William McKinley, later to be President, mayors, editors, publishers of ninety-three leading newspapers and religious periodicals, writers, clergymen, and prominent business leaders like John D. Rockefeller, J. Pierpoint Morgan and Charles Scribner.

The Blackstone Memorial states:

"What shall be done for the Russian Jews? It is both unwise and useless to undertake to dictate to Russia concerning her internal affairs. The Jews have lived as foreigners in her dominions for centuries, and she fully believes that they are a burden upon her resources and prejudicial to the welfare of her peasant population, and will not allow them to remain. She is determined that they must go.

"Hence, like the Sephardim of Spain, these Ashkenazim must emigrate.

"But where shall 2,000,000 of such poor people go? Europe is crowded and has no room for more peasant population. Shall they come to America? This will be a tremendous expense, and require years.

"Why not give Palestine back to them again? According to God's distribution of nations it is their home; an inalienable possession from which they were expelled by force. Under their cultivation it was a remarkably fruitful land, sustaining millions of Israelites, who industriously tilled its hillsides and valleys. They were agriculturists and producers as well as a nation of great commercial importance; the center of civilization and religion.

"Why shall not the powers, which, under the treaty of Berlin in 1878, gave Bulgaria to Bulgarians and Servia to the Servians now give Palestine back to the Jews?

"We believe this is an appropriate time for all nations, and especially the Christian nations of Europe, to show kindness to Israel. A million of exiles, by their terrible sufferings, are piteously appealing to our sympathy, justice and humanity.

"Let us now restore them to the land of which they were so cruelly despoiled by our Roman ancestors.

21

"To this end we respectfully petition His Excellency, Benjamin Harrison, President of the United States, and the Honorable James G. Blaine, Secretary of State, to use their good offices and influence with - and here the Memorial lists a dozen foreign leaders - to secure the holding, at an early date, of an International Conference to consider the condition of the Israelites, and their claims to Palestine, as their ancient home."

In the Memorial, Blackstone deliberately steered clear of any mention of Protestant theology. In the cover letter to President Harrison, just the final two paragraphs out of nineteen involve religious argumentation. Blackstone urges the President "to take a personal interest in this great matter" and secure through negotiations "a home for these wandering millions of Israel, and thereby receive to yourselves the promise of Him, who said to Abraham, I will bless them that bless thee, Gen. 12:3."

President Harrison formally received the Memorial and its author on March 5, 1891. And although Harrison did not act on Blackstone's proposal, he was obviously paying attention. A few months later, in his third annual address to Congress in December 1891, Harrison expressed his "serious concern because of the harsh measures now being enforced against the Hebrews in Russia...by the revival of anti-Semitic laws."

Press coverage of the Blackstone Memorial was favourable. *HaPisga,* the Hebrew periodical of the early Zionist *Hovevei Zion* (Lovers of Zion) wrote: "Let the Christians do whatever they can to help us in the resettlement in Palestine. As to the question of our faith, let that rest until Elijah returns and then we shall see whether or not their dream materializes."

Blackstone's Memorial was penned a full four years before Theodor Herzl (whom we meet in the next chapter) wrote *The Jewish State* in 1896. Herzl had never heard of Blackstone. But Blackstone was quick to recognize the significance of Herzl's book. He sent Herzl a bible, in which he highlighted all verses relating to Israel as the only viable homeland for the Jews.

We will return to Blackstone shortly. But first, we will cross the Atlantic and make the acquaintance of another William, the Reverend William Henry Hechler.

23

CHAPTER 3

The clergyman who helped to legitimize Herzl

Born in 1845 in the Hindu holy city of Benares, to a German Anglican priest father and an English mother, William Hechler attended boarding schools in London and in Basel. He quickly displayed his mastery of languages, and in additional to being bilingual in English and German, he also learned Hebrew, Greek, Latin, Arabic, Italian, Spanish, Portuguese, French and two African dialects.

Hechler's interest in Jewish studies and Palestine seems to have been influenced by European Evangelical Restorationist theology. Before long he was developing his own eschatological theories and timelines in which the restoration of the Jews in their ancient land played a major part.

He became an Anglican clergyman like his father, and served as a chaplain and medic in the German army during the Franco-Prussian war of 1870-1871.

In the early 1870s, Hechler was appointed household tutor to the children of Frederick I, Grand Duke of Baden. While working with the children, he got to know their favourite cousin, the young Hohenzollern prince who would later become German Kaiser Wilhelm II. When the Grand Duke's son Prince Ludwig died prematurely in 1876, Hechler accepted a position in County Cork, Ireland, where he married Henrietta Huggins. He returned to London in 1879 as an official minister of the Church of England.

In 1882, as Metropolitan Secretary of the Church Pastoral Aid Society, Hechler went on a fact-finding tour of Russia to investigate the situation of the Jews. He was horrified by the violent anti-Jewish pogroms in Russia. While in Odessa, he met Leon Pinsker, a Russian-Polish doctor, a former assimilationist, whose views changed radically after he witnessed the massive anti-Jewish riots in Tsarist Russia in 1881.

In 1882, Pinsker published an essay in German, *Selbstemanzipation (Auto-Emancipation)*, which argued for Jewish self-rule and the development of a Jewish national consciousness. "The Jews are not a living nation; they are everywhere aliens ….The proper, the only solution, is in the creation of a Jewish nationality, of a people living upon its own soil." Pinsker chaired the Jewish nationalist group Hovevei Zion, and his pamphlet would eventually be a landmark in Zionist history.

But because he was an East European Jew, rather than a more "sophisticated" Western European Jew, Pinsker's call for Jews to take control of their own lives with their own national solution, did not resonate far in 1882.

When Theodor Herzl wrote *Der Judenstaat* (The Jewish State) fourteen years later, he had never heard of Pinsker or the Hovevei Zion movement, and was totally unaware of the Russian experiments in Palestine. Because Herzl and his West European Zionists thought in political and diplomatic terms, and were less concerned with the practical aspects of colonization, they became known as the "politicals." East European Zionists were known as the "practicals."

Hechler, however, did know about Pinsker, and was probably influenced by him when he wrote *The Return of the Jews to the Land of Israel in accordance with the prophets* in 1884.

"It is the duty of every Christian to love the Jews," he wrote. The book called for the Jews to return to Palestine as a pre-condition for the return of Jesus, although conversion of the Jews to Christianity was not a pre-condition.

In 1885, Hechler was appointed Chaplain at the British Embassy in Vienna, a post he held for 25 years.

He was consumed with the question of the Jews and Palestine. In his private residence, he collected bibles and maps of Palestine, and he constructed a scale model of the Jewish Temple in Jerusalem. His Bible studies led him to calculate that a major event in 1897 or 1898 would lead to the Restoration of the Jews. Given that we now know that the first Zionist Conference was held in 1897, his calculations seemed to have been vindicated.

While perusing a Viennese bookstall in early March, 1896, Hechler happened upon Herzl's *The Jewish State*, published just a few weeks earlier.

Herzl was a staff writer for Vienna's Neue Freie Presse in Paris, and had covered the infamous trial of Captain Alfred Dreyfus, a Jewish French military officer falsely accused of selling French military secrets to the Prussians.

The background to the trial was that in October 1894, a cleaner in the German Embassy in Paris discovered a secret military document in the trashcan of the German military attaché. From the contents, it was clear that the classified document originated with a French officer. Although the evidence pointed to infantry officer Major Ferdinand Walsin Esterhazy, the French military authorities decided to scapegoat Dreyfus. He was an obvious and easy target - because he was a Jew.

Dreyfus' arrest triggered banner headlines. The anti-Semitic, nationalist newspaper La Libre Parole declared: *High treason! Jewish officer arrested! Captain Dreyfus!*

On December 19, 1894, Dreyfus attended a court-martial that was held largely in-camera. The military judges unanimously found Dreyfus guilty, despite the spurious evidence. He was convicted of treason, and given a life sentence.

In order to maximize the impact of the verdict, Dreyfus was publicly degraded in the courtyard of the Military College on the morning of January 5, 1895. In a ceremony designed to humiliate him in the eyes of all, he was stripped of his military rank, and exiled to Devil's Island.

On that January morning, Herzl was in a state of shock.

He had just witnessed the Parisian crowd braying for Jewish blood and shrieking "Death to the Jews." In a moment of clarity, he realized that Jewish assimilation to which so many Jews had clung to over the previous century was an illusion. He saw that the hopes of assimilationists like himself were unfounded.

Anti-Semitism was not a thing of the past, and it would not go away. Herzl knew all about anti-Semitism in Russia.

What shocked him about the vicious anti-Semitic yells of the Paris mob was that these were French, not Russian. They were citizens of one of the bastions of European culture.

If Pinsker had been prompted to write *Auto-Emancipation* by Russian anti-Semitism, Herzl was prompted to become a Zionist activist because of French anti-Semitism. In May 1895, he marked his entry into political Zionism when he wrote a stirring letter to Baron Maurice de Hirsch on the problem of anti-Semitism.

When Hechler picked up Herzl's *The Jewish State*, he read:

"The Jews who wish for a State will have it. We shall live at last as free men on our own soil, and die peacefully in our own homes. The world will be freed by our liberty, enriched by our wealth, magnified by our greatness. And whatever we attempt there to accomplish for our own welfare, will react powerfully and beneficially for the good of humanity."

Hechler became convinced that Herzl had been sent by God to lead the restoration of the Jews. Herzl was the Hebrew prophet who would prove Hechler's calculations. Hechler decided to track Herzl down.

On March 10, 1896, Herzl recorded in his diary his first meeting with Hechler.

"The Rev. William H. Hechler, chaplain to the British Embassy in Vienna, called on me. A likeable, sensitive man with the long grey beard of a prophet. He waxed enthusiastic over my solution. He, too, regard my movement as a "prophetic crisis" – one he foretold two years ago. For he had calculated in accordance with a prophecy dating from Omar's reign (637-638) that after 42 prophetical months, that is, 1,260 years, Palestine would be restored to the Jews. This would make it 1897-1898.

"When he read my book, he immediately hurried to Ambassador Monson (British Ambassador in Vienna) and told him: the fore-ordained movement is here! Hechler declares my movement to be a "Biblical" one, even though I proceed rationally in all points. He wants to place my tract in the hands of some German princes. He used to be a tutor in the household of the Grand Duke of Baden, he knows the German Kaiser and thinks he can get me an audience."

Less than a week later, Herzl went to see Hechler.

"Yesterday, Sunday afternoon, I visited the Rev. Hechler. Next to Colonel Goldsmid, he is the most unusual person I have met in this movement so far.

"He lives on the fourth floor; his windows overlook the Schillerplatz. Even while I was going up the stairs I heard the sound of an organ. The room which I entered was lined with books on every side, floor to ceiling. Nothing but Bibles. A window of the very bright room was open, letting in the cool spring air, and Mr. Hechler showed me his Biblical treasures.

"Then he spread out before me his chart of comparative history, and finally a map of Palestine. It is a large military staff map in four sheets which, when laid out, covered the entire floor. "We have prepared the ground for you!" Hechler said triumphantly. He showed me where, according to his calculations, our new Temple must be located: in Bethel! Because that is the centre of the country. He also showed me the models of the ancient Temple. He sang and played for me on the organ a Zionist song of his composition."

Herzl knew that for his plans to succeed, he needed access to the highest places. He still lacked legitimacy in the eyes of Jews and Gentiles alike. He also had no avenues for gaining access to the German royal family.

Meeting Hechler could not have come at a more opportune moment for Herzl, who believed that only the intervention of the world powers of Europe could achieve a Jewish state. Hechler held the key to gaining access to European heads of state.

Herzl continued in his diary.

"Next we came to the heart of the business. I said to him: I must put myself into direct and publicly known relations with a responsible or non responsible rule – that is, with a minister of state or a prince. Then the Jews will believe in me and follow me. The most suitable personage would be the German Kaiser. But I must have help if I am to carry out the task. Hitherto I have had nothing but obstacles to combat, and they are eating my strength.

"Hechler immediately declared that he was ready to go to Berlin and speak with the Court Chaplain as well as with Prince Gunther and Prince Heinrich. Would I be willing to give him the travel expenses? Of course I promised them to him at once. They will come to a few hundred guilders, certainly a considerable sacrifice in my circumstances. But I am willing to risk it on the prospect of speaking with the Kaiser.

"He considers our departure for Jerusalem to be quite imminent and showed me the coat pocket in which he will carry his big map of Palestine when we shall be riding around the Holy Land together. That was his most ingenious and most convincing touch yesterday."

Hechler and Herzl met in Karlsruhe. On April 23, 1896, Herzl wrote:

"The Grand Duke had received him immediately upon his arrival, but first wanted to wait for his privy-councilor's report on my Jewish State. Hechler showed the Grand Duke the "prophetic tables" which seemed to make an impression. When the Kaiser arrived, the Grand Duke immediately informed him of the matter.

Hechler was invited to the reception and to the surprise of the court-assembly the Kaiser addressed him with the jocular words: "Hechler, I hear you wanted to become a minister of the Jewish State."

Two days later, on April 25, 1896, Hechler brought a very nervous Herzl to a private audience with the Grand Duke. This was the first time that Herzl had met royalty. He proceeded to share his vision of political Zionism and his solution to the Jewish Question with the Grand Duke, who was very taken with Hechler's eschatological predictions and with Herzl's pragmatic solutions.

The Grand Duke became a lifelong advocate of Herzl and the Zionist cause, and promised to leverage his relationship with his nephew the Kaiser to effect a face-to-face meeting.

Hechler, now Herzl's close friend and confidante, helped Herzl to organise and convene the First World Zionist Congress in Basel, Switzerland, in August 1897.

Some 200 participants attended the congress in the Municipal Casino of Basel, chaired by Herzl. The Congress formulated a Zionist platform, known as the Basle Programme, which heralded the foundation of the World Zionist Organization. Delegates voted to create a National Fund to co-ordinate the purchase of land in Palestine, dry marshes, construct roads and plant forests.

Herzl gazes over a hotel balcony during the First Zionist Congress in Basle

The Basle Programme stated: "Zionism seeks for the Jewish people a publicly recognized legally secured homeland in Palestine."

Two non-Jews were invited to attend the Congress as non-voting delegates.

There was Hechler, and there was Henry Dunant, who 4 years later would receive the first-ever Nobel Peace Prize for his role in founding the International Red Cross Movement and initiating the Geneva Convention.

Herzl referred to his two friends as "Christian Zionists" – the first known occasion that this term was used.

Herzl later confided to his diary: "If I were to sum up the Basle Congress in one word which I shall not do openly, it would be: at Basle I founded the Jewish State."

Continuing his quest to facilitate an audience for Herzl with the Kaiser, Hechler turned to Germany's ambassador to Austria, Philipp-Fuerst-von-Eulenburg, whose wife had been a student of Hechler's, and who was a close personal friend of the Kaiser. Von Eulenburg and the Grand Duke of Baden persuaded the Kaiser that it was time to meet Herzl.

The Kaiser wrote to Hechler: "I have been able to notice that the emigration to the land of Palestine of those Jews who are ready for it, is being prepared extremely well and it is even financially sound in every respect. I am convinced that the settlement of the Holy Land will soon bring blessing to the land."

In early autumn 1898, the Kaiser commissioned Thomas Cook to organise a trip to Palestine where he planned to visit the German settlements and to rededicate Christ Church in Jerusalem.

When the Kaiser stopped in Constantinople for a State visit on October 15, 1898, before continuing on to Palestine, Herzl was finally granted a private audience with the Kaiser. "Tell me in a word what I am to ask the Sultan," the Kaiser told Herzl.

"A Chartered Company – under German protection," was Herzl's response. True to his word, the Kaiser raised the issue with the Sultan, but the latter refused to consider granting the Jews a charter to Palestine even in return for the Jews assuming the Turkish foreign debt.

At their meeting in Constantinople, the Kaiser had told Herzl of his detailed itinerary in Palestine. So on October 29, 1898, outside Mikveh Yisrael, a small Rothschild-funded Jewish agricultural college, Herzl and his party waited for the Kaiser to make a brief stop on his way to Jerusalem.

The man chosen by his fellow farmers to lead Herzl's honour guard was the young Eliezer Margolin, later to become the first Jewish commander of a Jewish fighting unit in Palestine for almost 2,000 years.

Herzl was favourably and emotionally impressed by Margolin, resplendent in Arab abaya and kaffiye, and the other strapping youngsters who welcomed him.

Herzl later recorded in his diary: "a cavalcade came galloping towards us ... twenty young fellows who put on a kind of fantasia, lustily singing Hebrew songs. Hedad they cried, and dashed away cross-country on their little Arab horses."

Herzl also recorded his meeting with the Kaiser.

"At nine o'clock a commotion on the highway, which was lined with a 'mixed multitude' of Arab beggars, womenfolk, children and horsemen, heralded the approach of the Imperial party. Fierce looking Turkish cavalry galloped by at breakneck speed, hurling threatening glares and brandishing still more threatening rifles at the crowd. Then the advance couriers of the Emperor. And riding among a grey-clad group, including several ladies, the Kaiser himself.

"I signaled the children's choir of Mikveh Israel to strike up 'Heil Dir im Siegerkranz.' I stood next to a plough and took off my cork-helmet. The Kaiser recognized me at a distance. It gave him something of a start, he reined in his horse where I stood, and pulled up across from me.

"I moved forward a pace or two and when he leaned down past the neck of his horse and held out his hand to me, I stepped close to the mount and stretched up my own hand. "He laughed and darted one of his imperious glances at me:

"'How are you?'

"'Thanks, Your Majesty; I am having a look at the country. And how has Your Majesty found the journey?'

"'Very hot! But the country has a future.'

"'It is still sick,' I said.

"'Water is what it needs,' he said, bending down, 'much water.'

"'Yes, Your Majesty, irrigation on a large scale.'

"He repeated: 'It is a land with a future.'

"Perhaps he said further things which have escaped me, for he stopped for several minutes. Then he held down his hand to me again, and cantered off.

"Then the Imperial procession once more got under way, to the refrain of 'Heil Dir im Siegerkranz' welling from the childish throats.

"The Kaiser drew himself up prouder still in the saddle, and saluted the hymn as, back in Breslau, he had saluted the statue of his grandfather.

"Among the retinue I recognized the Court-Marshall Eulenburg, who greeted me affably.

"The spectators at Mikveh Israel were altogether dumfounded. Some of them asked who it had been. The Rothschild administrators looked sullen and annoyed."

By openly and publicly stopping to speak to Herzl, the Kaiser became the first European leader to acknowledge Herzl as the leader of the Zionist movement.

Four days later, Herzl and the Zionist delegation who accompanied him, again met officially with the Kaiser in his encampment outside Jerusalem.

But this meeting was a rude awakening for Herzl. Not only had the Kaiser failed to obtain the requested concessions from the Sultan, but it was now clear to Herzl that the Kaiser had also lost any personal interest in the Zionist enterprise. Herzl was sure he had failed.

However, the world thought otherwise. The London Daily Mail wrote on Friday November 18, 1898:

"An Eastern Surprise: Important Result of the Kaiser's Tour. Sultan and Emperor Agreed in Palestine. Benevolent Sanction Given to the Zionist Movement. One of the most important results, if not the most important, of the Kaiser's visit to Palestine is the immense impetus it has given to Zionism, the movement for the return of the Jews to Palestine. The gain to this cause is the greater since it is immediate, but perhaps more important still is the wide political influence which this Imperial action is like to have.

"It has not been generally reported that when the Kaiser visited Constantinople Dr. Herzl, the head of the Zionist movement, was there; again when the Kaiser entered Jerusalem he found Dr. Herzl there. These were no mere coincidences, but the visible signs of accomplished facts."

The world press saw the bigger picture. They saw Herzl's meetings with the Kaiser as momentous and successful. Even without knowing of Hechler's role in facilitating the meetings, the media did not miss the historical import of the political legitimacy that this encounter brought to Herzl and to Zionism.

After Herzl returned from Palestine, he wrote *Alt Neuland (Old-New Land)*, describing the country as he saw it in 1898 and as he imagined it would be 21 years later.

He envisioned a land of great cities, farms, and gardens; of modern technological processes; a canal connecting the Dead Sea and the Mediterranean; the chemical wealth developed; a cooperative economic order; and relations of peace and amity with the Arabs.

Hechler remained a devoted friend and advisor to Herzl, and attended five Zionist Congresses. Hechler was also the last non-family member to be with Herzl before he died in 1904.

Hechler recorded Herzl's last words: "Greet Palestine for me. I gave my heart's blood for my people." Herzl had bankrupted his family, ruined his marriage, ruined his relationships with his children and destroyed his health for Zionism and the Jewish people. He had given everything he could.

Jerry Klinger claims that it is no exaggeration to say that without Hechler, Herzl could easily have remained an obscure, eccentric, minor Austrian newspaper columnist.

Shortly after Herzl's death, Hechler used his contacts to effect a pivotal meeting between Zionist leader Chaim Weizmann and Foreign Secretary Arthur Balfour, who would later be the author of the seminal Balfour Declaration in 1917.

In response to Balfour's question why the Jews were so intent on Palestine, Weizmann asked Balfour whether the British would settle for Paris instead of London. Balfour replied that the British currently had London but the Jews do not have Jerusalem. True, said Weizmann, but the Jews had Jerusalem when London was still a swamp.

Before he died, Herzl arranged for the Zionist Executive to recognize Hechler's contribution by paying him a small monthly pension.

On the silver anniversary of Herzl's death in 1929, Hechler wrote a short article for a book of remembrances. On January 30, 1931, an almost impoverished Hechler died alone in obscurity. His daughter, an Anglican nun, buried him in an unmarked grave in London's New Southgate Cemetery, without so much as a tombstone to say he even existed.

In 2010, Jerry Klinger initiated a quest to give Hechler the respect he deserved. Jerry tracked down Hechler's gravesite with the help of Rev. David Pileggi, rector of Christ Church in Jerusalem's Old City.

Through the International Christian Embassy in Jerusalem, Jerry got support from Christian organizations and the British Jewish community.

On January 31, 2011, 80 years and one day after Hechler's death, the heads of 23 Christian Zionist Organizations, representatives of Zionist organizations, the Knesset Christian Allies Caucus, the International Christian Embassy in Jerusalem, the Israeli Embassy, and other international participants, attended the ceremony in New Southgate Cemetery.

A letter from Ron Prosor, Israel's Ambassador to the UK, was read out:

"I am delighted to send my warmest wishes on the occasion of the dedication of Reverend William Hechler's gravestone.

"Britain and Israel enjoyed a friendship long before the establishment of the State of Israel, as a result of the committed efforts of British Christian Zionists. Marking Reverend Hechler's prominent place in the rich tradition of Christian Zionism in Britain, on the eightieth anniversary of his passing, is especially timely. The support he gave to Theodor Herzl is symbolic of the understanding that is found today among our Christian friends, of the eternal connection that exists between the Jewish People and Eretz Yisrael. The People of Israel deeply value your solidarity. You are friends who stand with us as we face the challenges of the future, who share with us a love of the Holy Land.

"I commend the work of all of the organisations involved in this important act of remembrance. Shalom Aleichem – may Reverend Hechler's memory be blessed."

The text on Hechler's tombstone reads:

When The Lord Shall Build Up Zion,
He Shall Appear in His Glory. Psalm 102:16
Rev. William Henry Hechler
01.10.1845 – 30.01.1931
A Lover of God, His Word
And His Ancient People
Tireless Adversary of Anti-Semitism
Friend and Counselor of Theodor Herzl
Has God Rejected His People?
By No Means!
Romans 11:1

CHAPTER 4
The Reverend and the Lord: Blackstone and Balfour

Let us return to Reverend Blackstone. While there is no record that he ever met Britain's Lord Balfour, Blackstone played a key role in facilitating the passage of the Declaration that bears Balfour's name.

In the short term, the Blackstone Memorial of 1891 had no immediate impact on American policy. But this did not prevent Blackstone from deepening his involvement with the Zionist movement.

The revised 1908 edition of *Jesus is Coming,* which had a print run of hundreds of thousands, reflects a shift in Blackstone's thinking. He describes the conditions of Jewish colonization and even mentions the completion of the railroad from Jaffa to Jerusalem as confirming scripture.

He wrote: "If Israel is beginning to show signs of national life and is actually returning to Palestine, then the end of this dispensation is surely nigh."

The new Zionist movement advocating resettlement of the ancient homeland "has certainly marked a wonderful innovation in the attitude of the Jews and a closer gathering of the dry bones of Ezekiel."

After spending five years in China, Blackstone returned to America in 1914. He sensed that Ottoman rule over the Holy Land was nearing an end.

On the other side of the Atlantic, Zionist leader Chaim Weizmann was having similar thoughts. Throughout WW1, British Zionism, under Weizmann's leadership, had been cultivating British political leadership in order to obtain a British declaration in favor of a Jewish homeland in Palestine.

Like Herzl, Weizmann believed that only the political clout of a major power could make Zionist aspirations in Palestine a reality. Herzl had appointed Germany to this role. Weizmann regarded Britain as the future protector of a Jewish homeland.

The British and American Zionist movements were very separate, and there was some quite unsubtle competition in the air.

In December 1915, American Zionist leader Louis Brandeis learned Weizmann was trying to persuade the British to make a declaration in favour of Jewish settlement in Palestine.

Even if Weizmann's pride did not let him ask Brandeis directly for help, Brandeis correctly understood that the British Zionists needed American Zionist support. Brandeis decided to act.

A close advisor and confidant to the Brandeis's inner Zionist circle was philanthropist Nathan Straus (after whom the Israeli city of Netanya is called). The Straus family owned Macy's. One of Nathan's brothers, Isidor, had perished aboard the Titanic in 1912. Another brother, Oscar, had been the American ambassador to the Ottoman Court under Theodore Roosevelt.

More significantly, Oscar had been a signatory of the 1891 Blackstone Memorial to President Harrison. In a curious twist of fate, Nathan's son became very friendly with a young German Jewish student, Otto Frank – the father of Anne Frank.

Nathan Straus brought the Blackstone Memorial to the attention of Brandeis. In April 1916, Brandeis wrote to US Secretary of State, Robert Lansing, enquiring what action had been taken on the Memorial.

Brandeis requested copies of all communications in relation thereto. "The document appears to me to one of great importance at the present time."

Just three months after the State Department claimed that the 1891 Blackstone Memorial had been "lost," Brandeis was confirmed as the first Jewish American to serve on the US Supreme Court. This gave him even greater leverage to argue the Zionist case, and he independently spent hours researching secondary and news media sources for information on the Memorial.

In May 1916, Nathan Straus contacted Blackstone on behalf of Brandeis: "Mr. Brandeis is perfectly infatuated with the work that you have done along the lines of Zionism. In fact he agrees with me that you are the Father of Zionism, as your work antedates Herzl".

In May 1916, Brandeis himself asked Blackstone to update and re-present the Memorial to President Wilson. "That document, ante-dating as it did Theodore Herzl's own participation in the Zionist movement, is destined to become of historical significance: and I trust that you may be as successful in securing support for this new Memorial as you were a quarter of a century ago. In view of the work being directly undertaken by the Jewish Zionist organization, your memorial would presumably be most effective if it derives its support from non-Jews."

Blackstone did not need much prompting. He decided that in addition to seeking individual signatories as he had done for the original Memorial, he would also secure support from organizations and churches.

He collected some new impressive signatures: the President of Cornell University, the Governor of California, and the Postmaster General.

Crucially, Blackstone secured the endorsement of the Presbyterian Church, knowing full well that President Wilson was a religious Presbyterian raised on the Bible. He read scriptures daily and prayed for guidance daily. Wilson would later say: "I am a son of the manse, son of a Presbyterian clergyman, and therefore am with you completely and am proud to think that I may in some degree help you rebuild Palestine."

Brandeis held back from presenting it formally to the President, since America was still neutral in the war between Britain and the Turks. Brandeis knew that public endorsement by the President of the Memorial could lead to retribution against Christian Missionaries and Jews in the areas of Ottoman control.

Brandeis asked Blackstone to be patient, and to await the best opportunity to formally present the Memorial. Blackstone agreed to let Brandeis determine when and where the Memorial would be most effectively used.

A year later, in May 1917, Brandeis was still hesitant, believing that any publicity around the Memorial was still unwise. Blackstone lost patience. He had his own route to the President. One of the signatories of the original 1891 Blackstone Memorial was William E. Dodge, the father of Cleveland Dodge, Wilson's Princeton classmate and close personal friend and advisor.

On 14 June 1917, Blackstone sent his Memorial directly to the President.

"In God's providence, it has been my privilege to secure a remarkable endorsement of the memorial in behalf of the Jews, which is presented herewith. It, as you will note, incorporates a former Memorial of the same character, which it was my privilege to present to President Harrison, twenty-six years ago.

"As the promoter of the memorial and representing the sentiments expressed in personal conferences with those who have endorsed it, I wish to emphasize that, because of unforeseen and changing circumstances, we all desire you, when taking action, to be guided by your best judgment as to the method or plan of accomplishing the main object asked, named to obtain relief and safety for the Jews of the world, and promote the realization of their God-given desire to be restored to their divinely appointed home Palestine.

50

"Believing that the progress of events augur the imminence of the psychological moment for benign action in behalf of the Jews, similar to that exhibited by Cyrus of Persia, and assured of your sympathy and willingness to aid the Jewish people in their present tragic sufferings, and praying that you may seize the opportunity of securing to yourself and our nation the blessing, promised by God to Abraham and his seed, by showing kindness to Israel I am most respectfully,

"Your obedient servant.

Two weeks later, Rabbi Wise informally presented the Blackstone memorial to President Wilson. Wise wrote to Blackstone that the President preferred that Brandeis should decide the timing of any formal presentation of the petition to him.

In fact, the Blackstone Memorial never did get formally or publicly presented to President Wilson. But there can be no doubt about the impact that the Memorial had on Wilson.

In early September 1917, the Balfour Declaration hung in the balance. Lloyd George's British War Cabinet demanded a statement of support from the Americans before proceeding. On October 16, 1917, Col. Mandel House acting on behalf of Wilson, cabled the British Government pledging America's support for proposed Declaration.

Wilson's endorsement was a key factor in Britain's decision to issue the Declaration. Wilson insisted that his approval should not be made public. He wanted to give the American Zionists the opportunity to ask him to approve the Declaration after it had been published.

Foreign Office,
November 2nd, 1917.

Dear Lord Rothschild,

I have much pleasure in conveying to you, on behalf of His Majesty's Government, the following declaration of sympathy with Jewish Zionist aspirations which has been submitted to, and approved by, the Cabinet

"His Majesty's Government view with favour the establishment in Palestine of a national home for the Jewish people, and will use their best endeavours to facilitate the achievement of this object, it being clearly understood that nothing shall be done which may prejudice the civil and religious rights of existing non-Jewish communities in Palestine, or the rights and political status enjoyed by Jews in any other country"

I should be grateful if you would bring this declaration to the knowledge of the Zionist Federation.

The Balfour Declaration was issued on November 2, 1917. Weizmann fully appreciated the critical importance of Wilson's support.

He wrote to Brandeis to acknowledge his help: "I need hardly say how we all rejoice in this great event and how grateful we all feel to you for the valuable and efficient help which you have lent to the cause in the critical hour. Once more, dear Mr. Brandeis, I beg to tender to you our heartiest congratulations."

"May this epoch-making be a beginning of great work for our sorely tried people and also of mankind."

Brandeis and Wise later acknowledged that what guaranteed the victory for the Zionists was not their greater diplomatic skills, but their success in appealing to Wilson's biblically-based Christian faith.

According to historian Paul Charles Merkley, the Blackstone Memorial had the effect of "firmly planting in many minds" the "notion of American sponsorship of a Jewish return to Palestine."

Merkley: "While it would be reckless to claim that we can trace a clear line of cause and effect from Blackstone's Memorial of 1891 to the creation of the State of Israel in 1948, it is not at all far-fetched to say that the Memorial is the place to go to find the clearest expression of the motivation that won President Woodrow Wilson, and which would continue to be the surest, the most constant source of American Christian Zionism."

Addressing a Zionist mass meeting in Los Angeles in 1918, Blackstone told his audience that he had been a Zionist for over thirty years because "true Zionism is founded on the plan, purpose, and fiat of the everlasting and omnipotent God, as prophetically recorded in His Holy Word, the Bible."

At American Zionist Conventions, Blackstone was singled out for special honour and recognition for his outstanding contribution to the Zionist movement. He remained a committed Zionist for the rest of his life. He spoke out actively and aggressively against anti-Semitism focusing in particular on the hatred spread by Henry Ford in his advocacy for the *Protocols of the Elders of Zion*.

He died in November 1935, and was buried, as modestly as he had lived, at Forest Lawn Cemetery in Glendale, California. The Chicago Jewish community and the Jewish National Fund raised funds to plant the William E. Blackstone forest in the Judean Hill in 1956.

We have seen how Hechler helped Herzl reach international respectability, and how Blackstone influenced the Balfour Declaration. Before we meet two more clergymen, we will make a detour to meet two Christian agricultural experts who also made their mark on the restoration of the Jews to their homeland.

CHAPTER 5

Elwood Mead and the need for a viable water plan

Elwood Mead was born in 1858, in the town of Patriot, Indiana. He studied the chaos of a non-existent public water policy in Colorado, and the private initiatives being undertaken to bring water to needed areas. He earned a reputation as an expert in the field, and developed a course in irrigation.

Hired by Wyoming as territorial engineer in 1888, Mead wrote the water code when Wyoming became a state in 1890. This code was used as the basis for new or revised water codes for many states, as well as for Australia, South Africa, Canada, and New Zealand.

From 1907 to 1915, Mead was Chairman of the State Rivers and Water Supply Commission for the state of Victoria, Australia. In 1915 he was appointed first Professor of Rural Institutions at the University of California. As head of the new California Commission on Land Settlements and Rural Credits, he created the State Demonstration Colony at Durham, California.

Professor Mead encountered several Jewish students from Palestine. They taught Mead the rudiments of Zionism, the Zionist agricultural settlements, and the problems that agriculture faced in Palestine. The Jewish students greatly impressed Mead with their diligence and desire to adopt his techniques of farm management.

In 1919, the Zionist leadership in Palestine sent Josef Wilkansky, head of the Zionist Commission's Agricultural Department in Jerusalem, on a study tour of the USA in search of information and techniques that would help Jewish settlers in Palestine avoid mistakes made by farmers in geographically similar areas in the United States. When Wilkansky toured state regulated farming in California, he visited Mead's State Demonstration Colony - and caught a glimpse of the future. Wilkansky got to speak to Mead, and told him that his expertise would be invaluable in Palestine.

By 1922, Mead's successes in Colorado, Wyoming, and California had generated a worldwide demand for his services. The Churchill White Paper, which we will meet in another chapter, linked future Jewish immigration to Palestine's "economic absorptive capacity." This made it urgent for the Zionist leadership to demonstrate the viability and potential profitability of Zionist settlements.

We have seen that the relationship between the British Zionists and the US Zionists was never smooth. But again Weizmann needed a favour from Brandeis: Could Brandeis persuade Mead to come to Palestine as soon as possible? Weizmann knew that the pragmatic Brandeis believed that modern businessmen methods must prevail over passionate speeches and abstract ideals.

Brandeis' understanding of the Balfour Declaration and the British Mandate was that the Zionist Organization's mission was more about economic development than political and cultural definition.

Weizmann rejected what he termed derisively as Brandeis' "Yankee Doodle Judaism." He regarded the economic development of Palestine as part of a wider agenda to demonstrate to the world that a Jewish homeland was both an economic and a political reality.

Fortunately, these philosophical differences did not prevent Weizmann from asking, nor Brandeis from facilitating. Knowing that Mead's expertise generated in the American west could really help establish a firmer Jewish foothold in Palestine, Brandeis persuaded Mead to visit Palestine as soon as possible.

Mead arrived in late 1923. Weizmann wanted Mead to "see everything" and make "suggestions unhampered and unfettered" by political debates.

Weizmann also undertook to adopt Mead's suggestions, whatever they may be. Weizmann's confidence in Mead proved correct. Mead's private and public assessments of Jewish colonization reinforced Weizmann's vision for Jewish development in Palestine, while at the same time giving Weizmann powerful ammunition in his political battles.

In private, Mead advised the Zionists to continue buying land in Palestine. Rounding out existing settlements meant more contiguous land holdings, which meant more efficient use of money and water. He proposed that land purchases in support of expanded settlements be confined to the Esdraelon, Jezreel, and upper Jordan valleys, since the coastal plain was already showing signs of over-development.

Mead was particularly concerned that groundwater supplies could be threatened by over-rapid growth and haphazard well-drilling. He believed that consolidation of Zionist settlements would also provide for more complete drainage and irrigation systems.

Mead wanted the Zionist leaders to adopt a more American-like businesslike approach. He told them that the keys to success were clear delineation of organizational goals, adequate capitalization of projects, strictly ordered budgets, contractual agreements, and competent business management.

Mead was convinced that Palestine had the potential of becoming as verdant as Southern California. The Jordan Valley, like California's Imperial Valley, had the capacity "to supply distant cities with fruits and vegetables."

Writing to Weizmann, Mead described the situation in Palestine:

"It is not paradise. You have handicaps, in the way of your neighbours, a government in a transition stage and poor, and the fact that your agriculture is small with small production, but in spite of all this you can overcome these obstacles by using your minds and concentrating energetically on the problems before you."

Mead particularly encouraged more extensive development of the upper Jordan Valley. He recommended the purchase and drainage of the Huleh basin as part of a plan to both develop the "hinterlands" and lay claim to the Jordan Valley's extensive water resources.

For Mead, the process and overall intensification of water development in the upper valley was linked to the overall development of urban and rural populations. The success of Zionist settlements, particularly coastal cities, depended on water from the Jordan Valley.

Weizmann strongly endorsed the Huleh idea, but any purchase, drainage, and development of the Huleh basin entailed complex negotiations. It would take another decade before further action was taken.

In the meantime, Weizmann had to deal with claims resulting from prior Ottoman concessions, with French desires to protect the rights of their subjects in Syria, and with British fears that endorsement of Jewish land purchases might provoke renewed Arab violence. Mead's recommendations influenced land purchasing and settlement strategies in the upper Jordan valley and agricultural development outside the valley, and eventually led to a significant increase in demands on the valley's water resources.

Weizmann's primary goal for the Zionist movement was the successful colonization of Palestine, rather than the organization of Jewish political and cultural agencies throughout the Diaspora.

Mead's endorsement of the Palestine colonization effort was therefore seen as a vote of confidence in Weizmann. Mead's capitalist ethos and strong critique of "communistic colonies" also influenced Weizmann's thinking. He accepted Mead's logic that Zionists had to decide between social experimentation and financial solvency. He also accepted Mead's financial forecasts of the potential returns on investments.

According to Weizmann's interpretations of Mead's estimates, a £1m investment in Palestine would yield £3m over ten years.

Mead's endorsement of the viability of Zionist settlement efforts in Palestine became an effective weapon in the Zionist armory. From now on, Mead would be cited whenever the future of Jewish immigration was linked to the demonstration of Palestine's economic absorptive capacity.

In a memorandum sent to Zionist leaders after his initial trip to Palestine, Mead pronounced

"I regard the Jewish Colonies in Palestine as the most important and valuable influence now being exerted in this country for the improvement of agriculture and the creation of a stable and enlightened rural life. The creation of new and larger settlements will stabilize social and political conditions in the country, as well as give a needed support to the present rapid development of cities and towns in Palestine. Apart from any question of religious faith or aspiration the movement to create rural Jewish settlements is deserving of world wide encouragement and support."

Mead not only sent confidential reports and memoranda to Weizmann and the Zionist leadership. He also publicly endorsed the Zionist programme.

In 1924, shortly after being appointed Commissioner of the US Bureau of Reclamation, Mead contributed a highly favorable review of Jewish settlements to The American Review of Reviews. In his article, *New Palestine,* Mead openly blamed Islam Ottoman governance for the demise of Roman irrigation systems that, according to Mead, had once supported "lands flowing with milk and honey."

Mead reserved his greatest praise for Zionist hydraulic engineering projects spearheaded by émigré Russian engineer, Pinhas Rutenberg. While studying in the USA, Rutenberg managed to complete detailed design of utilizing Palestine's hydraulic resources for irrigation and electrical power production. He served as head of the Haganah's Tel Aviv office during the anti-Jewish Arab riots of 1921, but his real passion was the economy.

Rutenberg's hydro-electric plant in Naharayim

If Weizmann and Ben Gurion embodied political Zionism, and Jabotinsky embodied military Zionism, Rutenberg embodied industrial Zionism. He convinced Colonial Secretary Churchill that a dam in the upper Jordan Valley would provide power and water for all the inhabitants of Palestine. Churchill told Parliament in 1920 that Rutenberg's efforts were evidence that Jews were taking positive steps to make Palestine more productive and therefore less of a drain on the British treasury.

Churchill shared Mead's view that if the Arabs of Palestine were left to themselves, they would never have taken effective steps toward the irrigation and electrification of Palestine.

Mead saw that Rutenberg's project would enable the Jordan Valley to support not only agriculture in the valley but industry and a higher standard of living throughout Palestine. A dam in the upper Jordan Valley would "light cities, turn the wheels of factories, pump water for irrigation, and give to the country a varied and prosperous industrial life."

Unveiling a parallel that would surface in future Zionist literature, Mead compared Zionist agricultural efforts in Palestine to contemporary American agricultural successes.

Mead proclaimed, "In their agriculture and rural life, these valleys in Palestine promise to be a replica of southern California .... The largest single irrigated area in California is the Imperial Valley, and its counterpart in Palestine is the valley of the Jordan."

Despite Mead's best efforts, Palestine's economic circumstances deteriorated. In 1927, Weizmann again turned to Mead, asking him to undertake a comprehensive survey of Zionist agricultural efforts in Palestine. Weizmann, the consummate politician, needed Mead's survey to help counter bad publicity, reinvigorate Zionist fund-raising efforts in the United States and Europe, and "create a real financial foundation for the future."

Weizmann arranged for Mead to visit Palestine between August and October 1927. Mead's second report, "Agricultural Colonization In Palestine," came as a shock to Weizmann. Mead recommended against the creation of any new Jewish settlements, and advised that a large percentage of the colonization efforts should be written off. Still convinced that Palestine could be made productive, and not wishing to see the Jewish effort in Palestine fail, Mead was concerned that publication of his report would produce "ill results" and "unsettle public confidence in those entrusted with responsible control."

Mead urged Weizmann to keep the report confidential, and to circulate it only as an internal document. Mead reminded Weizmann that the Palestine situation was not unique. "In 1924, the United States Congress wiped off $28,000,000 of the indebtedness of settlers on Federal reclamation projects .... "

In his formal reports to Zionist leaders and correspondence with British mandatory officials, Mead continued to praise the overall accomplishment of the Zionist movement in Palestine, and expressed himself optimistic about Palestine's capacity for supporting a larger population. Only Zionist "intelligence, science, and high purpose" could unlock the riches of the Huleh basin, he argued.

Recalling ancient Israel's biblical boundaries, Mead explained that contemporary Palestine and the Jordan Valley had been "reduced in resources to an extent that can only have a marked influence on what can be accomplished." It was crucial to ascertain the amount of water available and to develop it within all possible limits. Wise management could accomplish much with the as yet untapped potential of the Jordan Valley, the Jezreel Valley, and the coastal plain.

Implicit in Mead's assessments were the need for an overall water resources base including groundwater, river water and rainwater.

Water for agriculture, he argued, was only one part of the programme; Palestine's land-water nexus was in reality the critical foundation for a modern industrial state in which an economy's agricultural sector promoted an expanding industrial sector.

Mead knew that urban and industrial development depended on agricultural produce and water. Palestine's urban centers and factories were equally critical for agricultural economic development specifically and national economic development in general. He also believed that forestation efforts were essential. The hills overlooking the Jordan Valley had been denuded by combinations of neglect, warfare, and harmful Arab agricultural practices.

Mead's advice represented the confluence of three key principles: consolidation of settlements, intensification of agriculture, and wise management of people and production.

Weizmann's attempts to get Mead to visit Palestine for a third time coincided with violent clashes between Arabs and Jews in late 1929. Mead, however, faced his own problems in a USA now gripped by a worsening economic crisis. The economic depression in the United States and the construction of the Boulder Dam curtailed Mead's ability to directly assist Palestine, Jewish colonization, and his friend Weizmann.

66

Nevertheless, Mead remained actively engaged in an advisory capacity until his death in January 1936, particularly in the area of water law.

The ultimate validation of Mead's ideas on water law occurred with the passage of Israel's Water Law of 1959, which declared all waters, surface, groundwater, waste and drainage waters as well as flood waters, as public property and placed them under state supervision for "the development of the country."

In 1957, Israel completed the drainage of the Huleh Basin. In 1964, Israel began pumping water from the Jordan River to Israel's coastal and southern regions, just as Mead had envisioned. Mead was the first American water planner to envision the Jordan Valley as part of large-scale economic development program for Palestine. Water in the valley could not remain in the valley; its potential economic benefit was too great to be left underutilized. Mead saw that a modern Palestine, like a rapidly developing American west, required water from all available sources. The Jordan's waters were part of a much larger picture.

Another major contribution of Mead was that he opened a conduit between Zionists and American experts in the Bureau of Reclamation, Department of Agriculture, and the TVA. This technological conduit extended to valuable political leverage.

With the US State Department relatively indifferent to Zionist efforts in Palestine throughout the mandatory period, officials in other parts of the US Administration played an increasingly important role in American-Palestine relations.

The growing relationship between an emerging Jewish nation and Americans eager to duplicate American hydraulic institutions and practices in Palestine proved to be a major component of Mead's legacy.

Following Mead's death in 1936, the federal government decided to name the lake created by the Hoover Dam for him.

CHAPTER 6
Professor Walter Clay Lowdermilk, Zionist soil expert

"Food comes from the holy earth. The land with its waters gives us nourishment. The earth rewards richly the knowing and diligent but punishes inexorably the ignorant and slothful. This partnership of land and farmer is the rock foundation of our complex social structure."
W C Lowdermilk

If you walk around the campus of Haifa's famous Technion Institute of Technology, you will come across the Lowdermilk Department of Agricultural Engineering. The department is named in honour of its founder, Walter Clay Lowdermilk, Rhodes Scholar, eminent American soil conservation expert, Bible lover and fervent Zionist who served as Professor of Soil Conservation from 1954 to 1957.

In 1938 and 1939, as assistant chief of the US Soil Conservation Service, Lowdermilk made an 18-month tour of Britain, Holland, France, Italy, Algeria, Tunisia, Tripoli, Egypt, Palestine, Trans-Jordan, Lebanon, Cyprus, Syria, and Iraq, to study soil erosion and land use. This tour was sponsored by the Soil Conservation Service, in order to gather data from those areas - where some lands had been in cultivation for hundreds and thousands of years - that might be of value in helping to solve the soil erosion and land use problems in the USA.

Lowdermilk hoped to understand the factors that had led to the devastating Dust Bowl that hit the American Southwest in the 1930's. His special interest was how land was used by different populations throughout the centuries, and what the results of those practices had been. He was especially excited to travel to Palestine because there he would have as his historical roadmap the Bible - "the most authentic and longest written record of any nation except China."

Lowdermilk wrote that the movement for "a Jewish homeland in Palestine had begun four thousand years earlier when Abraham, prompted by divine inspiration, left the plains of Mesopotamia to establish a new people on the land of Canaan. ... On the rivers of Babylon, the exiled Jews continued to dream of returning to their devastated National Home."

Describing his first impression of arriving in Palestine, Lowdermilk expressed a deeply religious perspective: "In February, 1939, we, like the Children of Israel, left the land of Egypt before daylight. We crossed the southern part of the Land of Goshen, which Joseph had given to his brothers. We entered the Sinai Desert, where the Israelites and their flocks and herds had wandered for forty years."

During the Palestine expedition, Lowdermilk developed his vision for the economic rejuvenation of Palestine, particularly the development of the valley of the Jordan River. He argued that diverting the Upper Jordan and of the Yarmuk and Zerqa rivers into open canals running around the slopes of the Jordan Valley would facilitate the irrigation of the surrounding areas.

Lowdermilk was mightily impressed by what the Jews "who fled to Palestine from the hatreds and persecutions of Europe" had accomplished in a short period of time.

He was astonished to find 300 colonies "defying great hardships and applying the principles of co-operation and soil conservation, and demonstrating "the finest reclamation of old lands that I have seen in three continents." They did this "by the application of science, industry and devotion to the problems of reclaiming lands, draining swamps, improving agriculture and livestock and creating new industries."

Jewish settlers had successfully cross bred Dutch with local Syrian cows and produced a hardier breed suitable for the climate and more than tripled production. Orange trees cultivated by the Jews were yielding 200 per acre whereas California averaged 100-120.

On his return to the USA, Lowdermilk gave numerous illustrated lectures, and in 1942 he published a mimeograph called *Conquest of the Land Through Seven Thousand Years*. He described crossing into Palestine:

"We crossed the Jordan Valley ... and ... looked at the Promised Land as it is today, 3000 years after Moses described it to the Israelites as a land flowing with milk and honey. Where soils are held in place by stone terrace walls that have been maintained down to the present, we found the soils still cultivated after several thousand years and still producing -- not heavily, to be sure, because of poor soil management.

"Most important, the soils are still in place and will grow bigger crops with improved soil treatment. We also looked upon the glaring hills of Judea not far from Jerusalem, dotted with only a few of its former villages, whose terraces have been kept in repair for more than 2000 years.

"What is the cause of the decadence of this country that was once flowing with milk and honey? As we ponder the tragic history of the Holy Lands, we are reminded of the struggle of Cain and Abel, how it has been made realistic through the ages by the conflict that persists even unto today, between the tent dweller and the house dweller, between the shepherd and the farmer.

"The desert seems to have produced more people than it could feed. From time to time the desert people swept down into the fertile alluvial valleys where, by irrigation, tillers of soil grew abundant foods to support teeming villages and thriving cities. They swept down as a wolf on the fold to raid the farmers and their supplies of food.

"Raiders sacked and robbed and passed on, often leaving destruction and carnage in their path, or they replaced former populations and themselves became farmers only to be swept out by a later wave of hungry denizens of the desert.

"Conflicts between the grazing culture and farming culture of the Holy Lands have been primarily responsible for the tragic history of this region. Not until these two cultures supplement each other in cooperation can we hope for peace in this ancient land.

"We saw the tents of descendants of nomads out of Arabia who in the 7th century swept in out of the desert to conquer and over-run the farming lands of Palestine and again in the 12th century when they drove out the Crusaders. They and their herds of long-eared goats, often called cloven-hoofed locusts, let terrace walls fall in ruin and unleashed the forces of erosion which for nearly 13 centuries have been washing the soils off the slopes into the valleys to make marshes or out to sea.

"In recent times a great movement has been under way for the redemption of the Promised Land by Jewish settlers, who have wrought wonders in draining swamps, ridding them of malaria and planting them to thriving orchards and fields, in repairing terraces, in reforesting the desolate and rocky slopes, and in the improvement of livestock and poultry.

"The work of the Jewish colonies is the most remarkable reclamation of old lands that I have seen in three continents.

"Throughout our survey of the work of the agricultural colonies, I was asked to advise on measures to conserve soil and water. I urged that trees of orchards be planted on the contour and the land bench-terraced by contour plowing. So insistent was I on this point that finally we were told of one orchard that was planted in this manner.

"We went to see it. The trees were planted on the contour, the land was bench-terraced and slopes above the orchard were furrowed on the contour and planted to hardy trees. By these measures all the rain that fell the season before, one of the wettest in many years, was absorbed by the soil. No runoff occurred after this work was done, to cut gullies down slope and to damage the orchards below.

"When I asked where the man responsible for this had learned these measures, he told me that he had learned them at the Institute of Water Economy in Tiflis, Georgia, in Trans-Caucasia."

Lowdermilk argued that engineering miracles like the TVA demonstrated that wild waters could be harnessed to produce cheap power for industry and agriculture that would transform waste lands into fields, orchards, and gardens. This would enable the area to support a much larger population.

75

He believed the Jordan Valley would be viable for such a reclamation project and that it would even surpass what the TVA had done in the Tennessee Valley.

As he put it: "The Holy Land can be reclaimed from the desolation of long neglect and wastage and provide farms, industry and security for possibly five million Jewish refugees from the persecutions and hatreds of Europe in addition to the 1,800,000 Arabs and Jews already in Palestine and Trans-Jordan."

He proposed the development of a power programme, through the utilization of the deep incline of the Jordan River channel. He envisaged diverting seawater from the Mediterranean into the Jordan valley. Lowdermilk knew that 3 million people had inhabited Palestine in Roman times, and that the climatic conditions had not changed since then.

He believed that Jewish agricultural colonization had demonstrated the feasibility of restoring the soil. He saw a parallel between the climatic and geophysical conditions of Palestine and Southern California were very similar. In California, the problems of soil erosion and irrigation had been successfully tackled.

During his visit, Lowdermilk wrote and broadcast *The Eleventh Commandment* over the radio in Jerusalem.

He dedicated the broadcast to the Palestinian Jewish villages whose good stewardship of the earth inspired this idea.

"Thou shalt inherit the holy earth as a faithful steward conserving its resources and productivity from generation to generation. Thou shalt safeguard thy fields from soil erosion, thy living waters from drying up, thy forests from desolation, and protect thy hills from overgrazing by the herds, that thy descendants may have abundance forever. If any shall fail in this stewardship of the land, thy fruitful fields shall become sterile stony ground or wasting gullies, and thy descendants shall decrease and live in poverty or perish from off the face of the earth."

When Lowdermilk returned home, he presented his report to Vice-President Henry A. Wallace, who remarked that Lowdermilk "had become the most complete Zionist convert anyone could ask for."

Lowdermilk's attachment to the Zionist cause was matched by that of his wife Inez, his 'comrade and inspiration'. The daughter of a Methodist minister, she described herself as 'a Zionist born and bred'. Indeed, as one British diplomat who, after hearing Inez's outspoken support for Zionism, reported back to the Foreign Office, she 'obviously sees herself in the role of modern Old Testament Prophet'.

Lowdermilk became a leading member of the American Palestine Committee which was founded in 1941. He was also a member of the executive committee of the Christian Council on Palestine, formed a year later in 1942, with the goal of winning over to Zionism members of the clergy and makers of Christian opinion. Reverend John Grauel, who we will meet in a later chapter, was also a member of this Council.

Together with other committed Christian supporters of Zionism in the United States such as the theologian Reinhold Niebuhr, the philosopher Carl Friedrich and Senator Owen Brewster, Lowdermilk preached the Zionist position at conferences of Christian educators and clergy throughout the United States.

He also testified in support of Zionist claims before Congressional House and Senate Committees. His Zionist efforts were held in high regard by the American Zionist movement, and his scientific arguments were quickly adopted as a central plank of the Zionist programme.

In 1943, at the suggestion of Weizmann, the American Zionist Emergency Committee established a body of experts known as the Palestine Survey Commission, to examine the Jordan Valley proposals for increasing the Jewish population of Palestine. Lowdermilk was appointed to the board of the commission.

Lowdermilk's proposals became a foundation stone of the argument for a Jewish State. When Zionist leaders gave evidence before the House of Representatives' Foreign Affairs Committee in 1944, they all based their arguments on Lowdermilk's scientific findings and estimates that the land of Palestine could support at least 1.5 million more people, while an increase in industrial capacity would enable Palestine to support approximately 5 million more people.

Sometimes a book can have an unexpected impact on history. So it was with Lowdermilk's *Palestine, Land of Promise,* which against all odds became a best-seller. Not only did the book capture the Zionist imagination, but it made a significant impact on the economic, political and propaganda debate over Palestine during the dying years of British Mandatory rule.

Lowdermilk's belief in Palestine's economic potential carried much weight. The book was well received in scholarly journals and the general media. In March 1944, Senator Bennett C. Clark addressed his colleagues on behalf of a Jewish homeland in Palestine and the abolishment of the 1939 British White Paper which limited Jewish immigration.

Clark told his Senate colleagues that for the past few nights he had been up reading Lowdermilk's *Palestine, Land of Promise,* and he urged them all to do the same.

In Britain, Lowdermilk made an impression on the Zionist leadership, offering an opportunity to appeal to what they referred to as "the progressive gentile of today."

This was at a time when Brigadier General Sir Wyndham Deedes, the Rev. Dr James Parkes and Blanche (Baffy) Dugdale (Lord Balfour's niece) were all playing an important part in promoting the Zionist claims in the Gentile word.

Deedes, a former Chief Secretary of the Palestine administration between 1920 and 1923, was described by one of his anti-Zionist foes as '110% Zionist', and founded the British Association for the Jewish National Home in 1943.

Scholar and theologian, the Rev. Dr James Parkes, was viewed by Zionist leaders as 'eminently fitted to speak for what the volume of British opinion which has reached Zionism by way of Biblical study and grasp of what Judaism stands for in the world'.

Baffy Dugdale used her wide-ranging political and social connections to promote the Zionist cause, and even had a column in the *Zionist Review*, the weekly newspaper of the Zionist Federation of Great Britain and Ireland, aptly entitled 'Thru Gentile Eyes', in which she set out the reasons why non-Jews should support Zionism.

The publication of the British edition of Lowdermilk's *Palestine: Land of Promise* in October 1944 was an immediate success. It was by eminent commentators like George Orwell, who praised it in a review in the *Manchester Evening News* as a well-documented case for the achievements of Zionist settlers in Palestine.

The book was reprinted six times between in the space of two years. In 1945, the Information Department of the London Office of the Jewish Agency distributed 10,000 copies of Lowdermilk's book to 'appropriate sections of non-Jewish opinion'.

Weizmann even sent a copy to British Foreign Secretary Anthony Eden in 1944:

"I hope you will not think I am trying to force 'Zionist propaganda' on you – far be that from me! Dr Lowdermilk, the author of the book, is a distinguished scientist and one of the senior civil servants in the United States Agricultural Department. He is not a Jew ... the book is well-written, objective and up-to-date; it presents, particularly as regards the future, some aspects of the situation which are both original and practical."

Perhaps more than any Gentile Zionist of the era, Lowdermilk was seen as being fundamentally disinterested and objective with regard to Palestine.

Sir John Russell, writing in the foreword to the British edition of Lowdermilk's book, pointed out that 'like myself, he is not Jewish and can view the enterprise quite dispassionately'.

Lowdermilk make no secret of the fact that his plans were 'intended to increase the absorptive capacity of Palestine to a very marked extent'.

He understood, maybe before many others, that by the end of WW2, the economic and political future of Palestine had become completely intertwined.

Lowdermilk was invited to give evidence in the Washington hearings of the Anglo-American Committee of Enquiry, which we will discuss in a later chapter. His views were seen as such a threat by the British that they looked for an independent, nongovernmental body of experts to repudiate Lowdermilk's book. One member of the Committee calling Lowdermilk's evidence a 'highlight' of the hearings.

Lowdermilk never gave up his plan to promote his Jordan Valley plan in both the United States and England. In 1948, on the eve of Israel's declaration of independence, he undertook a six-week tour of England with his wife in order to promote Zionism and to raise money for the Jordan Valley project.

Once Israel achieved its independence, Lowdermilk offered his practical expertise to help in building up the fledgling state.

Between 1951 and 1952, he was a special adviser on soil erosion to the Government of Israel, and between 1954 and 1957, he was Professor of Soil Conservation at Haifa Technion, where he founded the Lowdermilk School of Agricultural Engineering.

Lowdermilk advised Israeli leaders and agriculturalists to seek technical assistance rather than direct food aid, so that Israel could become increasingly self-sufficient and technically proficient in agricultural production and machinery. One Israeli government Minister said: "We don't need powdered milk; we need Lowdermilk."

While he was in Haifa, he had the satisfaction of finally seeing work begin on his Jordan irrigation proposals. This later became known as the National Water Carrier.

Lowdermilk died in 1974 at the age of 85.

CHAPTER 7

The key documents that shaped the course of modern Zionism

The three best-known documents in modern Zionist history are Theodor Herzl's *Der Judenstaat* in 1896, which laid out the founder of the modern political Zionist movement's vision of a Jewish state; the 1917 *Balfour Declaration*, which spelled out Britain's commitment for the establishment of a Jewish homeland in Palestine; and the State of Israel's 1948 *Declaration of Independence*, which marked the culmination of the Zionist dream.

Herzl's epistle laid out the vision, the Balfour Declaration provided a political road map for achieving this vision, and the Declaration of Independence marked the realization of that road map.

We have already seen how the Blackstone Memorial of 1891 influenced the Balfour Declaration. This chapter will describe a series of (mainly) British documents covering the 19-year period 1920-1939.

The San Remo Resolution, 1920

The League of Nations was established on 28 June 1919, when 44 states signed the Covenant. The San Remo Conference in Italy was an international meeting of the post-WW1 Allied Supreme Council, held in April 1920. The four Principal Allied Powers of World War I - Great Britain, France, Italy and Japan, allocated Class "A" League of Nations mandates. The text of the San Remo Resolution reads:

"The High Contracting Parties agree to entrust, by application of the provisions of Article 22, the administration of Palestine …. to a Mandatory…. The Mandatory will be responsible for putting into effect the declaration originally made on November 8, 1917, by the British Government …. in favour of the establishment in Palestine of a national home for the Jewish people."

85

The Churchill White Paper, 1922

After the March 1921 Cairo Conference, Colonial Secretary Winston Churchill told a gathering of Palestinian Arab leaders: "It is manifestly right that the Jews, who are scattered all over the world, should have a national centre and a National Home where some of them may be reunited. And where else could that be but in the land of Palestine, with which for more than 3,000 years they have been intimately and profoundly associated?"

Yet by his de facto annexation of 80% of the Palestine mandate, Churchill had neutered much of the basis of the Balfour Declaration. In July 1921, Weizmann privately expressed his fears for the future of Zionism.

"The British Government is whittling down the Balfour Declaration, immigration has practically stopped, the bulk of the British Officers in Palestine are not in sympathy with the movement, and the Zionists are not getting those concessions which are necessary for the establishment of the Home of the Jews in Palestine."

Even Lloyd George, under whose premiership the Balfour Declaration had been issued, criticised the curbs placed by successive British governments on Jewish immigration to Palestine:

"The notion that Jewish immigration would have to be artificially restricted in order to ensure that the Jews should be a permanent minority never entered into the heads of anyone engaged in framing the policy. That would have been regarded as unjust and as a fraud on the people to whom we were appealing."

John Henry Patterson, the Christian commander of The Jewish Legion in WW1, and one of the six officers I wrote about in *Six Officers, 2 Lions and 750 Mules*, attacked Britain's policies in *With the Judaeans in the Palestine Campaign*. Patterson singled out the General Headquarters in Palestine for its unfair treatment of and anti-Semitic attitudes to the Jewish battalions:

"In the face of this announcement (the Balfour Declaration,) certain officials in the Holy Land acted as if this epoch-making declaration were nothing but a scrap of paper.... This local anti-Jewish feeling eventually culminated in the Jerusalem pogrom - when under British rule murderous native mobs ran riot for nearly three days within the walls of the city."

In June 1922, Britain issued an official interpretation of the Balfour Declaration in the Churchill White Paper, which introduced the concept of economic absorptive capacity. This concept became the valve by which the British regulated Jewish immigration, the valve over which Britain and the Zionists argued for years.

87

"For the fulfillment of [the Balfour Declaration] it is necessary that the Jewish community in Palestine should be able to increase its numbers by immigration. This immigration cannot be so great in volume as to exceed whatever may be the economic capacity of the country at the time to absorb new arrivals."

The British Mandate for Palestine, 1923

The Mandate officially came into effect on 26 September 1923. An early draft of the Mandate document contained a passage which read:

"Recognizing, moreover, the historical connection of the Jewish people with Palestine and the claim which this gives them to reconstitute it their national home..."

When this wording was rejected, Balfour suggested a draft that was accepted: "Whereas recognition has thereby been given to the historical connection of the Jewish people with Palestine, and to the grounds for reconstituting their National Home in that country ..."

Although the United States was not a member of the League of Nations, and was not legally bound to comment on the legality of the Palestinian Mandate, the US government entered into a bilateral treaty with Britain, the Palestine Mandate Convention, in December 1924.

The Shaw Report, 1929

Jews immigrated to Palestine at a trickle during the 1920s, moderated by economic absorptive capacity. But trouble brewed between Jewish settlers and the Arab indigenous population. Tensions simmered throughout the decade, boiling over in August 1929 in anti-Jewish violence at the Western Wall that spread to the rest of Jerusalem, to Hebron, and to other towns.

Following the 1929 riots, a commission of inquiry led by Sir Walter Shaw was sent to Palestine. The Shaw Report acknowledged the conflict inherent in the Mandate. The report pointed to the "racial animosity on the part of the Arabs, consequent upon the disappointment of their political and national aspirations and fear for their economic future."

The report recommended new measures for limiting Jewish immigration, and also recommended that a new study be carried out of the cultivation methods in Palestine.

"A National Home for the Jews, in the sense in which it was widely understood, was inconsistent with the demands of Arab nationalists; while the claim of Arab nationalism, if admitted, would have rendered impossible the fulfillment of the pledge to the Jews."

The Hope Simpson Report and the Passfield White Paper, 1930

John Hope Simpson came out to Palestine to follow up on the Shaw Report's request for a new inquiry on agriculture in the Mandate. The Hope Simpson Report called for the suspension of Jewish immigration until new agricultural methods made absorption of immigrants less burdensome on Arab peasants. The report ignored the capacity for growth in the industrial sector. As we saw earlier, this was the very question that Elwood Mead was addressing.

Published concurrently with the Hope Simpson Report, the Passfield White Paper of 1930 called for limits to Jewish immigration. The Passfield White Paper was authored by Lord Passfield, formerly Sidney James Webb, Fabian, socialist, and misguided supporter of the Soviet Union all his life. The books he wrote with his wife Beatrice, *Soviet Communism: A new civilization?* *(1935)* and *The Truth About Soviet Russia (1942)* were almost totally uncritical of Stalin's conduct during the extensive purges and the creation of the gulag system. Passfield's myopia extended to Palestine.

An angry Weizmann claimed that the Passfield White Paper was a concerted British effort to retract the promise made in the Balfour Declaration. He pressured the British government to reinterpret the White Paper.

In a letter to Weizmann, Prime Minister Ramsay MacDonald (urged on by his son and advisor Malcolm) repudiated the Passfield White Paper, and took as his yardstick the Churchill White Paper. He overturned the Passfield proposals, and the new metric of Jewish immigration became economic absorptive capacity.

The Report of the Peel Commission, 1937

In 1936, Palestinian Arabs launched a large-scale revolt against the Mandatory Authority. Recognising that they could not be everywhere at once, the Mandatory authorities authorised the formation of Jewish police units known as Notrim, also known as Jewish Supernumerary Police. Most Notrim were also members of the Haganah. An initial demand by the British that the Haganah be disarmed was dropped in the face of continued Arab violence.

The decision to arm, train, and pay Jews for military and paramilitary services in Palestine provided a perfect legal cover for the operations of Jewish underground groups. By July 1938, there were 22,000 Notrim. Russian army veteran Yitzhak Sadeh formed and trained a mobile patrol, "The Flying Squad," whose mission was to seek out and destroy Arab guerrillas operating near Jerusalem. This mobile force became the first officially sanctioned Jewish combat unit capable of independent offensive operations.

Soon after the Arab Revolt broke out, British intelligence officer Orde Charles Wingate, another of the six officers featured in my earlier book, was posted to Palestine. Arriving in Haifa in September 1936, Wingate openly espoused the Zionist cause, and obtained approval to train Jews in guerrilla warfare.

In response to the Arab Revolt, Britain sent the Palestine Royal Commission to Palestine, also known as the Peel Commission, to ascertain the reasons for the "disturbances."

The British failure to suppress the Arab Revolt turned a spotlight on the inadequacies of the mandatory regime. The commission represented the first time that the British Government had empowered an investigatory body to recommend major changes in the governance of the Mandate.

The Peel Commission arrived in Palestine in November 1936 and remained there until January 1937, hearing over 130 testimonies from Jews, Zionists, Palestine Arabs and other Arab nationalists. In January 1937, Ben-Gurion told the Commission: "I say on behalf of the Jews that the Bible is our Mandate which was written by us, in our own language, in Hebrew in this very country. That is our mandate. It was only the recognition of this right which was expressed in the Balfour Declaration."

Revisionist leader Zeev Jabotinsky told the Commission that the "demand for a Jewish majority is not our maximum - it is our minimum." He warned that three to four million European Jews would soon be seeking a safe haven in Palestine. He wanted all territory in the original 1920 British Mandate over Palestine - encompassing both banks of the Jordan River – to be part of the Jewish homeland.

Wingate also addressed the Commission, and explained why he favoured the establishment of a Jewish state:

"Nowadays people seem to imagine that impartiality means readiness to treat lies and truth the same, readiness to hold white as bad as black and black as good as white...I believe that righteousness exalteth a nation and righteousness does not mean playing off one side against the other while you guard your own interests."

Although leading Zionists distrusted British policies in Palestine, many of them continued to believe that the key to nationhood lay with the British. At a dinner in February 1937 to commemorate 20th anniversary of the founding of the Jewish Legion, Jabotinsky said that he still believed that there was a community of interests between Britain and the Jews. Later that year, he said:

"We may have a number of grievances against England but the English government is and will be the government of a well-disposed mother. England always puts obstacles in our way and always helps us."

In its Report, the Peel Commission claimed that the Mandatory Authority had contributed to the Jewish-Arab conflict. The Report suggested limiting Jewish immigration to 1,000 per month, restricting land sales to Jews, and the decolonization of British Palestine. The Commission proposed to partition the land into two states, Arab and Jewish, with Britain remaining as the Mandatory Authority over a small corridor that included Jerusalem and Jaffa, allowing access to the Mediterranean.

The Jewish state would cover an area in the North— twenty percent of the total, corresponding with existing areas of Jewish settlement. The Report supported establishing a Jewish national home in Palestine, envisaging an absorptive capacity of the Jewish state at no greater than one million persons.

"We should be able to give to the Jews all the dignity of a state, instead of merely a Jewish National Home. We should get rid at one blow of all ambiguity about the difference between Palestine as a Jewish Home and a Jewish Home in Palestine; all that bundle of controversy and difference would be swept away."

The Jews of Palestine expressed their willingness to negotiate with Britain on the basis of the Peel partition plan. Palestine's Arabs responded by resuming the Arab Revolt. Colonial Secretary Ormsby-Gore supported the Peel Report's call for partition. Foreign Secretary, Anthony Eden, opposed it.

Both men addressed Parliament in November 1937. Eden feared the response of Muslims in the Arab world to a Jewish state in Palestine fathered by Britain. He claimed that Jewish immigration had created the problem in Palestine, and partition would serve no purpose other than to find a destination for Eastern and Central European Jews seeking refuge from anti-Semitism.

For Eden, the Jews of Palestine were "foreign immigrants from outside [Palestine], who are, in fact, and setting aside for a moment Old Testament associations, as alien to present-day Palestinians as the Greeks to Asia Minor and the Moors to Spain."

Ormsby-Gore asked his fellow MPs: "On what grounds could we justify to the Jews the repudiation of a Statement of Policy issued only four months ago, and the offer to the Jews, in place of a settlement by partition, which follows inevitably from acceptance of the arguments and conclusions of the Royal Commission, of a permanent minority position in Palestine?

"I know of no new development which would provide us with a defence against the charges of betrayal which would be leveled at us from Jews throughout the world."

The Woodhead Commission, 1938

In 1938, the Woodhead Commission reversed the findings of the Peel Report. Partition was unworkable, it said, since it was impossible to establish a Jewish state that would not contain a sizeable Arab minority.

The St. James Conference, 1939

This conference was a futile attempt to make progress, and failed to find common ground.

Britain decided to clarify its position once and for all by issuing the infamous 1939 White Paper, which we discuss in the next chapter.

CHAPTER 8

The White Paper, May 1939

As Lloyd George himself pointed out, the way Britain had interpreted her commitment to a Jewish national home differed from the spirit of the Balfour Declaration. Nevertheless, prior to 1937, Britain continued to support the dual Zionist aims of Jewish immigration and colonization.

But once the Arab Revolt resumed, Britain started re-examining its pledges made to Zionists two decades earlier. The change in policy was encapsulated in the White Paper of May 1939.

The White Paper introduced three measures: immigration quotas for Jews arriving in Palestine; restrictions on settlement and land sales to Jews; and constitutional measures that would lead to a single state under Arab majority rule, with provisions to protect the rights of the Jewish minority.

The Zionist leadership interpreted the White Paper as a blatant betrayal of Britain's promises. The Jews could never accept that Palestine's Jewish community would remain a permanent minority that would never be allowed to exceed 33%, with land laws restricting the growth of Jewish settlement.

Under the terms of the White Paper, 75,000 immigration certificates would be granted to Jews over a five-year period. Considering that the White Paper was published long after the dimensions of the Jewish refugee crisis in Europe had reached critical level, the cynicism – not to mention the anti-Semitism – of the drafters of the White Paper can only be described as staggering.

Some British statesmen believed that 75,000 visas to Palestine were ample contribution towards the plight of Jewish refugees. Because war broke out less than four months after the White Paper was published, these immigration quotas were never filled during the war.

Thousands of Jewish refugees to Palestine in the first year of WW2 were detained, or, in the most extreme case, deported to the reaches of the colonial empire, because they did not possess the correct documents or because they had come from "enemy" territory. Over the course of the war years, the White Paper was rigidly and literally enforced.

Instead of discouraging the Zionists, the White Paper made the Zionist leadership more determined than ever to encourage clandestine immigration to Palestine. Ben-Gurion's opposition to the White Paper is immortalized in his oft-quoted phrase from September 1939:

"We must support the war against Hitler as though there were no White Paper, and fight the White Paper as though there were no Hitler."

The sense of betrayal was exacerbated by the fact that the White Paper's principal author was Malcolm MacDonald, who had advised his father Ramsey to repudiate the Passfield White Paper.

But once Malcolm was reappointed Colonial Secretary in May 1938, he underwent a sea change. The sense of betrayal led to increased Zionist support for a Jewish state covering all of Palestine, previously the view exclusively of Jabotinsky and the Revisionists. Moderates were now calling for this solution.

The Land Regulations, 1940

Based on the White Paper, Land Regulations divided Palestine into three zones: a zone where land sales to Jews were permitted, a zone where they were restricted, and a zone where they were prohibited. By upholding zones of Jewish population density, the British actually encouraged these areas to become more heavily populated by Jews.

The Harrison Report, 1945

In June 1945, US President Truman sent Earl G. Harrison to visit the Displaced Persons (DP) camps in Europe. Harrison reported: "The main solution, in many ways the only real solution, of the problem lies in the quick evacuation of all non-repatriable Jews in Germany and Austria, who wish it, to Palestine. The evacuation of the Jews of Germany and Austria to Palestine will solve the problem of the individuals involved and will also remove a problem from the military authorities who have had to deal with it."

The Report of the Anglo-American Committee of Inquiry, 1946

Based on Harrison's Report, Truman wrote to new British prime minister Atlee on 31 August, 1945.

"It appears that the available certificates for immigration to Palestine will be exhausted in the near future. It is suggested that the granting of an additional 100,000 such certificates would contribute greatly to a sound solution for the future of Jews still in Germany and Austria, and for other Jewish refugees who do not wish to remain where they are or who for understandable reasons do not desire to return to their countries of origin. No other single matter is so important for those who have known the horrors of concentration camps for over a decade as is the future of immigration possibilities into Palestine."

To counter Truman's request for 100,000 immigration certificates, Atlee agreed to a committee of inquiry. In November 1945, Truman and Bevin announced simultaneously that the US Government accepted the British proposal for the establishment of a joint Anglo-American committee of inquiry to examine the question of European Jewry, and "to make a further review of the Palestine problem in the light of that examination." Truman revealed that following his August 31 letter, the British Government said that:

"... it was not in a position to adopt the policy recommended, but that it was deeply concerned with the situation of the Jews in Europe." The same day as the announcement, Bevin said he expected the outcome to be a new constitution for Palestine, "not as a Jewish State but as a Palestinian State."

The committee was co-chaired by a federal judge from Texas, Joseph C. Hutcheson, and Sir John Singleton. The twelve members of the committee held hearings in Washington, London, Cairo, and Jerusalem between January and March of 1946. Their terms of reference were to "examine political, economic, and social conditions in Palestine as they bear upon the problem of Jewish immigration and settlement therein and the well-being of the peoples now living therein."

Members of the Committee took the Balfour Declaration and the Mandate as given. The most pressing issue for the Committee was whether or not to overturn the immigration quotas introduced by the 1939 White Paper and still in force. One of the experts who testified before the Committee was Professor Lowdermilk, who told them that the land in Palestine could indeed support its growing population.

Bevin announced that he would implement a unanimous report. After deliberating in Lausanne, Switzerland, the Committee signed their report on April 20, 1946.

The Report was a harsh indictment of the 1939 White Paper. Although the Committee advocated a binational state, it supported parity, rather than the Arab majority rule that underpinned the White Paper.

"We know of no country to which the great majority can go in the immediate future other than Palestine. Furthermore, this is where almost all of them want to go. There they are sure that they will receive a welcome denied them elsewhere. There they hope to enjoy peace and rebuild their lives."

The Report described the illegal immigration efforts of the Jews:

"The Jewish organisations are actively engaged in these operations, carried out latterly by the purchase or charter of ships for voyages from southern Europe, in the absence of effective control of embarkation.

"Armed clashes are liable to arise from the efforts to prevent interference; a number have arisen from the search for illegal immigrants and arms. Moreover, as recent incidents directly concerned with illegal immigration, may be cited the sabotage of patrol launches, and attacks on coast-guard stations."

The Report included strong words for those who would keep the 100,000 out of Palestine:

"Those who have opposed the admission of these unfortunate people into Palestine should know that we have fully considered all that they have put before us. We hope that they will look upon the situation again, that they will appreciate the considerations which have led us to our conclusion, and that above all, if they cannot see their way to help, at least they will not make the position of these sufferers more difficult."

On April 30, 1946, Truman unilaterally announced support for the transfer of 100,000 Jewish displaced persons to Palestine, ignoring the Anglo-American Committee's other nine recommendations. For Truman, the certificates were probably not unconnected with his bid for the approval of Jewish voters in the lead up to the 1946 Congressional elections.

While the Committee was drafting its report, the clandestine immigration movement had its first brush with the international media.

On April 3, 1946, 38 hijacked British military trucks were intercepted near the harbor at La Spezia near Genoa, Italy. The arresting Italian authorities had been alerted by the British to expect to find Fascists fleeing to Spain. However, on the trucks were 1,040 Jewish refugees, en route to the *Fede*, the ship that had been assigned to convey them to Haifa. As soon as they were arrested, the Jews declared a hunger strike.

Support for the hunger strike spread across the refugee camps in Italy. Jewish leaders in Palestine also supported the hunger strike. The Western media covered events in La Spezia closely - five articles appeared in the *New York Times* in April and May 1946. Finally, the refugees were permitted to sail together to Palestine.

The month-long La Spezia protest was a test run for an even bigger attempt to exploit the international media.

In the next chapter, we will describe in detail this even bigger attempt which unfolded the following year.

CHAPTER 9
4,515 Jewish passengers – and 1 Christian clergyman

In early 1947, 20-year-old Brooklyn native Nathan Nadler was strolling through Manhattan when he was accosted by Barney Ross. Born Dov-Ber Resofsky, Barney was a former American lightweight, welterweight, and junior welterweight boxing champion, and a decorated WW2 veteran.

Barney was also a recruiter for the American League for a Free Palestine (better known as the Revisionist Bergson Group affiliated with the Irgun Zvai Leumi - National Military Organization. Barney and his friends planned to form a "George Washington Legion" that would fight against the British in Palestine.

Attracted by the prospect of fighting alongside someone as illustrious as Barney, Nathan signed up.

He went for an interview, and a few days later, he was instructed to proceed to a pier in Baltimore to join the crew of the *SS President Warfield*.

The steamship was named after S Davies Warfield, the president of the Warfield Steamship Company. Warfield's niece was Wallace Warfield Simpson, "that woman" who was the reason that Edward abdicated his throne. Most people are very familiar with this steamship – under a different name: *Exodus*.

When Nathan reached the pier in Baltimore harbour where the *Warfield* was berthed, he climbed a rope ladder to the ship. As he clambered over the side, he was shocked that the first person to greet him was a Christian clergyman "with a clerical collar, a black tunic, and a big cross on his chest about eight inches high."

Who was this clergyman? Why was he helping the Haganah? And what was he doing on the *Warfield?* The answer is closely tied with what happened following the publication of the Report of the Anglo-American Committee of Inquiry.

In February 1947, despite Bevin's promise to implement any unanimous recommendations, the Atlee government made a public statement that Britain's Mandate in Palestine had become "unworkable," and that Britain was returning the mandate to the United Nations, which had inherited it from the League of Nations.

The British were confident that if the partition issue reached a vote in the United Nations General Assembly, it would fail, given that both the United States and the Soviet Union would have to support it, together with non-Western nations. The likelihood of getting past the required two-thirds majority seemed very slim.

During April and May 1947, a special session of the United Nations General Assembly met to consider the Palestine situation. These meetings determined the specific role and constitution of UNSCOP, the United Nations Special Committee on Palestine, which would investigate conditions in order to recommend and implement a solution to the Palestine stalemate. The Zionist leadership knew that the establishment of a Jewish state depended hugely on what recommendations UNSCOP would make.

They also knew that a majority of UNSCOP members were decidedly unsympathetic to Zionist aspirations.

And then a miracle happened - UNSCOP recommended the partition of Palestine and the establishment of a Jewish state.

Future Prime Minister Golda Meir knew exactly what swung the committee round:

"The testimony and advocacy of this man for the creation of the Jewish state fundamentally and positively changed UN support for the creation of Israel."

"This man" was Reverend John Stanley Grauel – the guy with the clerical collar who welcomed Nathan Nadler aboard the *Warfield*.

Nathan was one of several hundred idealistic New Yorkers who risked their lives to participate in the struggle for Jewish statehood. If you ever take a stroll along the sidewalk outside 14, East 60th Street in the heart of Manhattan, you will notice a plaque: "This building sheltered the clandestine mission of the "Haganah," Israel's pre-state defense forces, which labored unceasingly for Israel's independence and survival."

In its day, the basement level of this building housed the famous *Copacabana* nightclub, which hosted some of the leading performers of the time: Frank Sinatra, Lena Horne, Jerry Lewis and Dean Martin.

A few floors above the nightclub was Hotel Fourteen, a residential hotel owned by Fanny and Ruby Barnett, both passionate Zionists.

Hotel Fourteen was dubbed 'Kibbutz Fourteen' by Ben-Gurion, who ran a weapons pipeline from the US to the Holy Land. The hotel was also the headquarters of Teddy Kollek, head of the American branch of the Haganah, and later the long-serving mayor of Jerusalem. One day, Kollek was having difficulty bribing a captain of a ship filled with arms that needed to be smuggled into Palestine.

He confessed to Sinatra what he was up to, so Sinatra decided to lend a hand and personally delivered the bribe money to the captain. Awed that Sinatra was asking *him* for help, the captain took the bribe, and the ship set sail for Palestine.

Kibbutz Fourteen was the nerve centre of the Haganah operations. And it was here that someone had the brainwave of recruiting the Reverend John Grauel to the cause.

John Stanley Grauel was born in 1917 in Worchester, Mass. He remembers his mother as a deeply religious woman with a mystical attachment to Jews.

"As I was growing up, she frequently observed that anyone on the side of the Jews would survive any of life's vicissitudes because the Jews were God's Chosen People. She was convinced Judaism must survive because it was the root of her own faith. It is my own deep conviction that the death of Israel would be the death knell of Western Civilization."

Working as a pastor to a small poor group of communities before WW2, he followed the news from Germany. "I was very distressed by pictures on the papers of Nazi thugs standing over old Jews scrubbing the streets of Berlin.

"While suffering this abuse and other indignities, the Jews were wearing their Iron Crosses won in defense of Germany during World War I.....Perhaps I was more sensitive to what was happening to the Jewish community because of my friendship with Judge Joseph Goldberg of Worcester. He was vice president of a national Zionist organization. In answer to my questions he gave me books to read on Zionism and awakened my interest in the search for a Jewish homeland."

Grauel asked his friend Goldberg how he could help.

Goldberg sent him to Dr. Carl Herman Voss, the founder and leader of the American Christian Palestine Committee, a national organization formed in 1946 as a merger between the American Palestine Committee and the Christian Council on Palestine. Voss was a Congregational minister, and a highly vocal advocate of the partition of Palestine.

In his book, *This is Israel*, Voss wrote: "No people in history has shown more fervent an attachment to a particular geographic area than the Jews have shown toward Palestine."

Voss offered Grauel the position of executive director of the Philadelphia office of the American Christian Palestine Committee, and he immediately started meeting Zionist leaders on a regular basis.

Grauel attended a Zionist conference in Princeton, N.J., where Rabbi Stephen Wise reported that at least seven hundred thousand Jews had been murdered by Hitler.

"For me the most electrifying portion of that conference was when David Ben Gurion spoke.... Later on I was introduced to Ben Gurion and sat around among others just listening to him. I caught an occasional reference to the Haganah, but it had no particular significance for me at the time....

"When I returned to Philadelphia, I began to be aware of the stream of young men going in and out of the next office....I went into the office and asked the man there, who introduced himself as Bucky Karmatz, what business he was in."

Bucky was running a recruiting office for the Haganah in the USA. Of course, he knew exactly who Grauel was:

"Talking to Bucky, I knew I had found my niche. I would join the Haganah, the underground, to become a part of that organization to rescue those who could be helped to leave Europe."

Grauel continued to function as executive director of the American Christian Palestine Committee in public, while in private he was raising funds to buy weapons.

One day in late 1946, Bucky came to Grauel with an invitation which would change Grauel's life forever. Bucky asked Grauel to join the crew of a ship that would attempt to break the British blockade and take refugees from Europe to Palestine.

In November 1946, the War Shipping Administration had sold *President Warfield* to the Potomac Shipwrecking Co. of Washington, D.C., not knowing that the latter were acting as clandestine purchasing agents of the Haganah.

The ship was towed to Baltimore, Maryland for refitting. One of the reasons the Haganah chose this particular ship was for its shallow draft. They planned for the ship to run close to the Sinai and Palestinian shoreline in waters that would be dangerously shallow for the larger, deeper hulled, British warships.

The Haganah invited Grauel to join the crew of the *Warfield* because they wanted a Gentile on board to report the truth of what happened. The Haganah correctly surmised that the word of a non-Jew would be believed more than the word of a Jew.

In order to facilitate his mission, Grauel obtained something that was almost impossible for any Jew to obtain. He managed to obtain legal permission to enter Palestine.

"One of the members of the Board of Directors of the American Christian Palestine Committee was Guy Emory Shipler, editor of *The Churchman*, an independent Episcopal magazine. My good friend Dr. Carl Voss, Executive Director of the committee, contacted Shipler before I left home, and they created a job for me as foreign correspondent for *The Churchman* with the appropriate credentials. That would make it possible for me to go ashore, should the crew of the Warfield-Exodus be caught and interned, which was always a possibility with Haganah ships.

"I would simply be regarded as having been aboard the ship as an observer and as such, not likely to be held with the others. Once on shore I would be available to make a full eyewitness report of the voyage."

Grauel moved to Baltimore where the *Warfield* was berthed, and the crew spent long days scrubbing, sanding, polishing, and mending. Most of them stayed in a local hotel, but Grauel was confined to the ship because he had been lecturing nationally for the last four years, and there was a chance someone would recognize him and ask embarrassing questions.

Grauel was not the only clerical crewman among the 43 crew members. Leon Reinharth was studying to be a Reform rabbi, and David Starec was studying at Yeshiva University to become an Orthodox rabbi. After the voyage of the *Exodus*, they both went on to fight in the battles for Jerusalem in the War of Independence.

Grauel: "About a week before we did sail, a ceremony took place on board. The crew and some important guests gathered as the crew took the Haganah oath. We were each given a sweater and a bible, Old Testament for everyone else, New Testament for me, which I regarded as very thoughtful.

"A few people were asked to say a few words, which I did in terms of an incident during WW2.

'Some soldiers were bivouacked somewhere in Italy, near a monastery. One Friday night they decided to hold Sabbath services in the monastery garden. To hold religious services Jews must have a minyan, that is, ten Jewish men. Having only nine, they looked around and spied a statue of Jesus and remembering He was Jewish, they held their services."

The *Warfield* left Baltimore on February 25, 1947, and made its way across the Atlantic. During the voyage, the crew celebrated Passover.

"Prayers were said, the traditional questions of the seder were asked and answered, and suddenly I found myself close to tears. The reader has recited the traditional words, 'Next year in Jerusalem.' Here I was, a country preacher, a Methodist seated aboard a rolling ship in the mid-Atlantic with a group of Jewish chaverim (friends) in celebration of the self-same festival Jesus celebrated so many years before. What made the moment even more moving for me was that we were on our way as instruments of deliverance in assisting those of the second Exodus to return to their land, Eretz Israel."

When the *Warfield* reached Marseilles, Grauel travelled to Paris to arrange a visa from the British Consulate. This would enable him to enter Palestine legally.

116

After being tipped off that he should make his way speedily back to Marseilles, Grauel discovered that the *Warfield* had had to leave in a hurry. He donned his clerical outfit to go to the British consulate in Marseilles to collect his visa, and the Haganah quickly got him on board another ship, *Hatikvah*, which rendezvoused with the *Warfield* in Portovenere, Italy.

"The British authorities in Rome had taken steps in cooperation with the Italian authorities to prevent the sailing of an unnamed vessel, which was to be used to transport 'escaping criminals and fascists,' the newspaper reports ran.

"I was enraged to the point of tears many times by the lying statements of British officialdom in their undeclared war against the world's dispossessed."

After being prevented from leaving for some weeks by the Italian navy, the *Warfield* sailed into Port du Bouc, France, on July 9, 1947, where 172 trucks were waiting, loaded to capacity with Holocaust survivors.

"We had moored a large barge alongside the ship so that it would be possible for them to climb the side ladder to board. They moved forward gradually, looking up at the ship, some of them somewhat mystified. A little girl started up the ladder on to the side of the ship, and clambered over the top.

"I reached down to assist her. Under normal circumstances it would have been hard to distinguish her from any other girl her age. But I reached for her left elbow, there on her arm I could see the number, the mark of the concentration camp. She smiled her thanks for my aid and walked on as I stood there, chilled by what I had seen on that child's arm."

Once again, behind the scenes Britain tried valiantly to prevent the ship from sailing. Once again, the Haganah leadership on board outwitted the British, and the ship set sail for the Mediterranean voyage.

Conditions on board were terrible, and the ship's primitive sanitary facilities were soon overwhelmed by passengers suffering from sea sickness, dehydration and diarrhea. More than 400 pregnant women were on board.

"At dawn of the second morning, the loud-speaker announced: "Our first child has been born. Mother and child are in excellent health."

On July 17, 1947, as the *Warfield* sailed off the Sinai coast, she was officially given her new name: the *Exodus*. The Zionist leadership had deliberately timed this huge illegal operation to coincide with the presence in Palestine of members of UNSCOP, then on their fact-finding mission.

At 10 pm, a special broadcast, relayed from the *Exodus* to Kol Yisrael, the Voice of Israel, was carried to the world. Grauel had been asked to prepare a short appeal directed to the UNSCOP delegates who were meeting in Kadimah House, Jerusalem. He gave the following statement:

"Gentlemen, at this time we request you, in assembly in Eretz Israel, that you appear to gather testimony from the forty-five hundred Jews who are coming to Palestine in a few hours aboard the Exodus 1947. We remind you that no committee was called to witness the death of six million Jews in Europe. This is your opportunity to fulfill the requirements of your declared justice in these matters.

"Witness if you will the heartache, the sorrow, and the suffering and the utter brutality inflicted on our people by the British. They have acted as the Nazis have acted. They clubbed and shot down in cold blood our women and children. These British are imprisoning our people in the same types of camps on Cyprus as they suffered in Hitler's Europe. "You have declared yourselves to guarantee equal opportunity to all who seek freedom. Bear witness in truth to that declaration and hear our case now. We urge you to come and see our ship and to sit in judgment upon the British who we believe are doing the very thing that the United Nations has pledged itself to destroy."

On the night of July 18, while the *Exodus* was still in international waters 20 nautical miles off the coast of Gaza, British destroyers rammed the defenseless ship.

Everyone was thrown to the deck. Tear gas grenades were flying and exploding. British sailors boarded the *Exodus*, clubbing everyone in sight, and attacking with guns, stun grenades and bludgeons. As Grauel watched the Jewish youngsters defending themselves, he had an epiphany: "I was born and nurtured with the precious milk of freedom. I knew, I just knew I was watching the rebirth of a nation."

At one point, Grauel went into the chart room aft of the bridge where he was confronted by a British sailor wearing a gas mask. Grauel yelled, "I'm an American correspondent. I must get into the captain's cabin. There's a man seriously injured in there." The sailor responded: "Get out or I'll kill you." He swung at Grauel with his club, and Grauel fell backwards through the port. When the sailor threatened Grauel with his pistol, Grauel made his getaway.

The deck of the *Exodus* was littered with wounded and dead. First mate William Bernstein, a U.S. sailor from San Francisco, was bludgeoned to death in the wheelhouse. Two young refugee passengers were murdered; one was shot in the head.

A 15 year boy, the last survivor of the Yakubowitz family from the Holocaust, was shot in the stomach and killed. At least 150 refugees and crew members were injured, many severely.

With water beginning to pour in the holes in the walls, the Haganah leaders were worried that the ship would capsize with huge loss of life.

The *Exodus* limped into Haifa. When the thousands of refugee passengers caught their first glimpse of Palestine, they spontaneously lined the decks and sang Hatikvah, the Zionist Anthem.

Hundreds of British police and soldiers crowded the area. Cameramen took pictures from an overhead crane.

Also present to see this sight - as the Haganah had planned - were UNSCOP's Chairman, Judge Carl Sandstrom of Sweden, and Dr. Karel Lisicky from Czechoslovakia.

When the *Exodus* docked, Grauel noticed a stretcher being carried towards a tent at the end of the wharf. On it was the body of young Hirsch Yacubovich, who had been shot dead in the stomach six hours earlier. The blanket was down around his waist so it would appear as though he were still alive.

Grauel yelled, "That is the most goddammed despicable trick I have ever seen pulled."

His anger and agitation succeeded in drawing British attention to him. He was arrested, removed from the ship, interrogated in Haifa police headquarters, placed under house arrest, and sent to Haifa's Savoy hotel accompanied by two armed guards. As planned, his cover as an American correspondent had succeeded in getting him off the ship.

At the Savoy, the desk clerk informed Grauel that the bar was full of newspaper reporters. Before the police escort could stop him, he dove through the door of the bar.

The British had kept news about the *Exodus* under wraps. Grauel changed that instantly by loudly announcing that he was from the *Exodus* and would answer questions. Flash bulbs began to pop, and he was hemmed in all around by reporters as he gave them an eyewitness report of what had really happened.

At some point, a reporter edged in closer to Grauel and whispered the Haganah code word for the day. The reporter told Grauel to make his way to the men's room while the police were back at the doorway. Two Haganah operatives rushed Grauel out the back door and into a waiting American Press car.

122

Grauel crouched down in the back of the press car as the vehicle sped away. Teddy Kollek and the Haganah had engineered Grauel's escape so that he could fulfill his meticulously planned role. After a few hours in a safe house in Haifa, the press car took Grauel on a harrowing ride, past checkpoints manned by tanks, climbing its way up the winding road to Jerusalem. Grauel was taken to the Eden Hotel where he gave an impromptu press conference, and was then spirited away to Kadimah House to the apartment of the Ambassador from Guatemala, Jorge Garcia-Granados.

"I was introduced as a Haganah volunteer from the Exodus and while I sat down to catch my breath, Sr. Garcia-Granados called Dr. Victor Hoo, assistant Secretary General of the United Nations who was also in Kadimah House, and an appointment was made for me to tell my story the next morning."

Garcia-Granados described that first meeting with Grauel in *The Birth of Israel, the Drama as I saw it:*

"I was at home when the doorbell rang. Two American journalists stood at the entrance, accompanied by a stranger, tall and blond, in his thirties, with blue eyes, who appeared to be tense and anxious, wearing clothes that were obviously borrowed from someone else since they were not his size:

123

"'I would like to introduce the Reverend John Grauel of Worcester, Massachusetts', said one of the journalists as he propelled the pastor inside and closed the door behind him. 'He was a volunteer on the Exodus', continued the journalist, 'and we have rushed him here from Haifa - the British have been trying to jail him'. We would like you to hear his account before he places himself under the protection of the American Consulate.'"

The next morning, Grauel met UNSCOP in Dr. Sandstrom's quarters. Present were UN Secretariat members Dr. Hoo, Ralph Bunche, Garcia Robles, and UNSCOP members Ivan Rand, Canada (more about him in the next chapter), Enrique Rodriquez Fabregat, Uruguay, and Nicolas Blom, Netherlands.

They questioned him closely about his claim that the *Exodus* was not in territorial waters when the British attacked. Luckily, Grauel had the ship's log to verify his statement. He gave a full account of the battle, emphasizing the fact that the Jews had no weapons.

Grauel made one closing statement: "I have watched these people. I know what they are. And I tell you, the Jews in the European Displaced Persons camps insist on coming to Palestine, they will come to Palestine, and nothing short of open warfare and complete destruction will halt them."

Grauel had fulfilled his mission. The Haganah's strategy of placing Grauel on the *Exodus* had paid off.

"There was great gratification for me in knowing that my eyewitness report was now a matter of record. Inherent in the nature of the relationship between Christians and Jews was the fact that because I was a Christian, in this situation my testimony would be given greater credence than that of a Jewish crew member."

After giving his testimony to the UNSCOP delegates, Grauel was taken to an apartment house, and told to go up to the second floor and push the button. "I did as I was told and Golda Meir answered the door. It was her apartment. A meeting was being held there of the Jewish Agency.

"They asked me for a full detailed report of the Exodus trip from beginning to end and when I was finished, Golda was in tears."

Grauel stayed a few more days in Jerusalem, and after more hassles from the British authorities, he finally left on an American ship for New York. Just nine days after he arrived aboard the *Exodus*, Reverend John Grauel returned home. In New York, a large contingent of the press corps awaited him, eager for his story.

The New York Times reported: "Crew man from the Exodus 1947 denies the British met firearms; Grauel, on arrival in New York, says naval boarding party shot at Jews whose weapons were potatoes, canned goods."

Meanwhile, the British transferred the *Exodus* passengers to three deportation ships which left for Port-de-Bouc, where the Jews refused to disembark. After three weeks, during which the prisoners on the ships rejected offers of alternative destinations, the ships sailed to Hamburg, Germany, then in the British occupation zone. The Jews were sent to DP camps in Am Stau near Lübeck and Pöppendorf.

The irony of the situation seems to have been lost on the British – Jews who had escaped being murdered by the Nazis were now back on German soil.

As soon as he arrived back, Grauel threw himself back into clandestine Zionist activities aimed at getting crucial military and medical aid through to Palestine.

He spent the next thirty years heavily involved in speaking on behalf of Israel. He tirelessly lobbied politicians and church leaders, and maintained close relationships with many of the people he had met in Kibbutz Fourteen in New York, people who were now running the newly independent State of Israel.

Grauel was a frequent visitor to Israel, often paying for his passage by serving as a chaplain on board Zim ships that plied the US-Israel route.

He also became involved in the plight of Jewish communities in North Africa, and he was one of the first people to lead groups of young people to visit Holocaust sites in Europe.

Grauel died in Roosevelt, New Jersey in 1986. In accordance with his wishes, he was buried in the American Christian Missionary Alliance Cemetery on Emek Refaim Street, Jerusalem, in September 1986.

The Alliance cemetery was established by the American Presbyterian Church in the nineteenth century, and was originally known as the American Protestant Cemetery. In 1927, the Christian Alliance Church assumed full ownership of the cemetery, and renamed it in the early 1990s. In an area just 30 yards wide and 100 yards long, are some 400 graves of men and women, most of them Christians, some of them heroes, who bound their lives with the Jewish people and the State of Israel.

At the graveside ceremony, an Israeli flag was draped over Grauel's coffin, and the grave was flanked by an Israel Navy honour guard, *Exodus* shipmates, veterans of other immigrant ships, and representatives of B'nai B'rith and the American Jewish Committee.

Grauel's tombstone is inscribed with a verse from the Jerusalem Talmud:

"He who saves a single life...is as if he had saved the entire world."

The State of Israel recognized Grauel through the Humanity Medal and the Fighter for Israel Medal. Teddy Kollek, Grauel's Haganah colleague in New York and later mayor of Jerusalem, awarded Grauel the Medal of Jerusalem.

CHAPTER 10

The Reverend and the Justice: Hull and Rand

The UNSCOP delegation that left for Palestine consisted of representatives from 11 nations: Australia, Canada, Czechoslovakia, India, Guatemala, Iran, Netherlands, Peru, Sweden, Uruguay and Yugoslavia.

UNSCOP existed from 15 June to 1 September 1947. The delegates made a 2,200 mile 15-day tour of Palestine, a five-day trip to the Lebanon and Syria, a one-day visit to the King of Transjordan in Amman, and a 2,700 mile 7-day tour of DP camps in Germany and Austria.

The Committee held 13 public hearings in the course of which 37 persons representing 6 Arab states and 17 Jewish organizations gave evidence. The Committee also held 4 private hearings.

Some 200 correspondents were accredited to UNSCOP.

The Committee's tour of Palestine comprised Christian, Jewish and Moslem shrines in Jerusalem, the Hebrew University, Haifa, the Dead Sea, Hebron, Beersheba, Gaza, the Negev, Ramle, Jaffa Tel Aviv, Ramallah, Nablus, the Galilee, Acre and Rehovot.

We saw in the last chapter that the arrival of the *Exodus* was timed to coincide with the presence in Palestine of UNSCOP. We saw how John Grauel addressed some UNSCOP delegates in Jerusalem and told them the truth of what had happened.

This is our cue for introducing our fourth Christian clergyman.

Reverend William Hull was born in 1897 in the Canadian town of Winnipeg, where he became an ordained minister. During a church service, at Winnipeg's Zion Apostolic Church, he received a "calling from God."

With his wife Lillian, Hull moved to Jerusalem in 1935, and opened a small shop selling bibles, first in the Arab section of Jerusalem, and later, when Arab rioting forced them to seek refuge in the Jewish area of the city, on the "Street of the Prophets."

Hull had a very wide circle of acquaintances. He published a small-circulation periodical, *The Voice of Zion*.

Hull was the only Canadian Christian then living in Jerusalem – which is how he got to meet the Canadian delegate on UNSCOP, Supreme Court Justice Ivan Rand.

Canada's prime minister Mackenzie King was disinclined to have Canada involved in the Palestine debate, and was content to let the British govern Palestine and cope with the problems there. He did not relish Canadian involvement in an increasingly violent conflict. But when Britain thrust the Palestine question into the lap of the United Nations, Truman pressured Canada to be part of a commission of "smaller powers with no history of Middle East interest" to recommend a resolution to the question of Palestine. The British not unnaturally assumed that Canada would be sensitive to British interests.

Rand had only scant information on the problem of Palestine, the Jewish people, the disaster that had decimated European Jewry, and the urgent necessity for survivors to reach a safe haven in Palestine.

In order to keep Rand neutral, the Canadian Department of External Affairs provided him with a background paper that spoke of "two great historic tragedies... one Arab, the other Jewish," providing details of the Muslim defeat by the Mongols as a counterweight to the Holocaust.

When Rand arrived in Jerusalem in June 1947, he was delighted to discover a fellow Canadian. Reverend Hull became his. Hull later wrote about how Britain tried to isolate UNSCOP in Kadimah House.

"The building was in rather a remote location so that the movements of the inquiry members could be more carefully watched and the members guarded from outside contacts. They were treated more as the members of a murder-trial jury rather than as a commission sent to view the land and its problems. The Government was not so much concerned with the safety of the members as it was to keep outside voices from reaching their ears".

If this was the intent of the British, it did not work. Rand arranged to have dinner with Hull away from prying British eyes.

"During dinner he was full of questions, which I answered to the best of my ability and experience. He had already tasted something of the underhanded means used by the Government to frustrate the work and discovery of the Committee and as a Britisher he was angry at the unsportsmanlike, un-British tactics. Details of my experiences in connection with other anti-Jewish, pro-Arab Government acts added fuel to the flame which continued to burn brighter the longer he stayed in Palestine.

"This latter fact, however, was not known to me until some two year later when we met again in Ottawa, Canada. By then Mr. Justice Rand had become a strong Zionist and the State of Israel had already come into existence."

Evidence of Hull's impact on Rand can be seen in the foreword Rand wrote for Hull's book, *The fall and rise of Israel: the story of the Jewish people during the time of their dispersal and regathering:*

"It was a relief, then, when shortly after my arrival I had the good fortune to meet the author of this book. Here he was a Canadian... a clergyman who, for a number of years, had been carrying on a mission in Jerusalem: who was as I saw at once, a man of good will, well known to and knowing the many religious and racial groups in that amazing galaxy of rivalries and antagonisms.

"Here, I thought, was one whom I could trust to express himself with honesty and frankness. Somewhat to my surprise, I listened to words of high admiration for the Jewish people, their standards of life and the tremendous work they had done since returning to their ancient homeland. This sympathetic attitude released within me a vague constraint of doubt, uncertainty and puzzlement which, I see now, the limited and one-sided acquaintance I had had to that time with the Palestine question had generated.

"The controversy at once appeared unclouded by irrelevancies and shadowy prejudices and became one for decision in the light of subtle appreciations and comprehensive understandings."

In his Preface, Hull explains his motivation for writing the book:

"....so that the historical background leading up to, and the events which secured the establishment of the new State of Israel, may be more generally known. History, whether recording a punishment or a blessing, is the fulfillment of prophecy, and this point has been uppermost in my mind while writing this book."

Not content with his direct contacts with Rand, Hull also submitted his own letter to UNSCOP, setting forth the powerful case for Biblical Zionism.

While in Palestine, Rand also had first-hand contact with several former Canadian Jews who impressed him with their sincerity and devotion to the Zionist cause. One example was Mrs. M. Bloomstone of Kibbutz Ein Hashofet, who invited Rand to visit her on the kibbutz's 10th anniversary celebrations. Former Canadian Molly Lyons Bar-David invited Rand to a Shabbat meal. In her letter, she explained her reasons for coming to Palestine:

"I couldn't resist the challenge of Palestine and couldn't divorce myself from the fate of my people in Europe, nor ignore the implications of both; this, despite the fact that I was happy in Canada and (except for isolated occurrences and childhood sorry memories) was in no need for personal salvation."

Rand received a letter from Bernard Joseph, a Canadian lawyer who had arrived in Palestine in 1922. He was a leading member of the Palestine bar, and a future Minister of Agriculture. Joseph noted Rand's recently published essay on Brandeis. Rand admired Brandeis, a fellow graduate of Harvard Law School and a specialist in business and commercial law.

Rand also received a letter from Moshe Novomeysky, one of Palestine's leading industrialists and managing director of Palestine Potash Ltd., which had the concession for processing chemicals from the Dead Sea. Novomeysky had met Rand when UNSCOP visited the Dead Sea plant, and asked if they could meet again.

Novomeysky planned to build a railway to the Mediterranean. He was also a member of the Brandeis group set up to explore investment opportunities in Palestine. Before becoming a Canadian Supreme Court judge, Rand had been lead counsel for Canadian National Railways, and was naturally interested in railway projects.

UNSCOP members visiting a kibbutz

Another person connected with railways was David Horowitz, the Jewish Agency liaison with UNSCOP, and later governor of the Bank of Israel. One day, UNSCOP visited an Arab cigarette factory. The owners did not permit Jews on the premises, so Horowitz had to wait outside. This offended Rand.

He was even more shocked inside, where he discovered terrible working conditions, including the exploitation of child labour.

During UNSCOP's visit to the Negev, Rand commented on the Zionists' irrigation techniques: "Here you have a very strong argument on your behalf."

In the next chapter, we will see how Rand influenced the final report of UNSCOP. Without Rand, it is unlikely that UNSCOP would have so persuasively recommended to the UN General Assembly the establishment of a Jewish state.

Without this recommendation, it is unlikely that the Zionists would have obtained the two-thirds majority vote they required in the General Assembly in November 1947 in order to make statehood a reality.

Without Reverend John Grauel, it is unlikely that UNSCOP members would have been so sensitive to the suffering of the Jews.

And without Reverend William Hull, it is unlikely that Rand could have asserted his authority over the UNSCOP delegates.

CHAPTER 11

The Report of UNSCOP: The United Nations Special Committee on Palestine

UNSCOP meetings and discussions were never made public. Most of what we know about their secret deliberations was unearthed by Canadian lawyer John Ross who discovered Rand's UNSCOP papers at the University of Western Ontario Law School, where Rand was the Dean.

On July 28, 1947, all the members of UNSCOP travelled to Geneva to start drafting their report. Although UNSCOP had earlier decided that it did not need to visit DP camps in Europe, Grauel's impassioned plea in Kadimah House seems to have worked. A subcommittee left Geneva on August 8, visiting DP camps in Germany and Austria. They met American and British officials in charge of DP affairs, as well as officials of the Preparatory Commission of the International Refugee Organization.

The sub-committee also visited the children's camp of Indersdorf (near Munich), the Landsberg (Bavaria) camp comprising about 3,000 DPs and refugees, the camp of Bad Reichenhall (near Berchtesgaden) comprising about 5,000 displaced persons, infiltrees and refugees, the Rothschild hospital in Vienna which sheltered about 4,100 refugees, the camp of Dueppel (Berlin), and the camp of Hohne (near Belsen) comprising about 9,000 displaced persons and 1,800 infiltrees. Altogether, the sub-committee interviewed about 100 individual DPs.

In Geneva, UNSCOP delegates were divided on what they envisioned for Palestine. On August 27, 1947, only four days before the final report was due, the Swedish chairman Sandstrom realized that there were "too many different proposals" and that "the upshot would be a disjointed, incoherent, and from the point of view of the assembly, largely unintelligible report."

It was at this point that Rand stepped in. Taking control of the discussions, he persuaded his colleagues to reconsider their personal positions. He urged them to make every effort to find a solution which would avoid meeting fully the claims of one group at the expense of committing grave injustice against the other. A unitary Arab state, he told his colleagues, would be "a betrayal of the Jewish people and a violation of international agreements."

Rand personally headed the drafting sub-committee that worked on the final report. He persuaded the others to give the Jewish state control over the Negev, and he single-handedly reaffirmed the legality of the Balfour Declaration. He suggested that it was the White Paper of 1939, with its restrictive limits on Jewish immigration, that was the illegal document and the real source of the problems in Palestine.

At its forty-ninth meeting on 29 August 1947, UNSCOP unanimously approved eleven recommendations to the General Assembly, including the termination of the Mandate for Palestine at the earliest practicable date; and a short transitional period preceding the independence in Palestine, during which the authority entrusted with the task of preparing Palestine for independence shall be responsible to the United Nations.

Recommendation VI stated that the General Assembly should undertake immediately the initiation and execution of an international arrangement whereby the problem of the distressed European Jews, of whom approximately 250,000 are in assembly centers, would be dealt with urgently to alleviate their plight.

But on the question of partition, UNSCOP failed to achieve unanimity.

Canada, Czechoslovakia, Guatemala, the Netherlands, Peru, Sweden and Uruguay, influenced by Rand's arguments, expressed themselves in favour of the Plan of Partition. Whereby independence was to be granted to each State only after it had adopted a constitution complying with United Nations principles.

Britain was required to admit into the borders of the proposed Jewish State 150,000 Jewish immigrants. The Committee expressed its view about the Jews:

"Here are the sole remaining representatives of the Semitic race. They are in the land in which that race was cradled. There are no fundamental incompatibilities between them. The scheme satisfies the deepest aspiration of both: independence. There is a considerable body of opinion in both groups which seeks the course of co-operation.

"Despite, then, the drawback of the Arab minority, the setting is one from which, with good will and a spirit of co-operation, may arise a rebirth, in historical surroundings, of the genius of each people. The massive contribution made by them throughout the centuries in religious and ethical conceptions, in philosophy, and in the entire intellectual sphere, should excite among the leaders a mutual respect and a pride in their common origin."

The representatives of India, Iran and Yugoslavia, presented a minority recommendation for a unitary independent federal State of Palestine, comprising an Arab state and a Jewish state.

Rand's proposal eventually garnered support from a majority – 7 out of 11 – of the delegates

Justice Ivan Rand

Yoav Gelber, a member of the Jewish Agency negotiating team attached to UNSCOP: "In Geneva, Mr. Justice Ivan Rand dominated the Inquiry Committee's proceedings ... it was his resolution for partition which carried the day and brought concrete results."

In the next chapter, we will follow the progress of the UNSCOP Report in New York.

CHAPTER 12

Flushing Meadows and Tel Aviv Museum

When you say Flushing Meadows today, most people – especially sports fans – think of the venue where the US Open tennis tournament has taken place since 1978.

But for anyone interested in modern Jewish history, Flushing Meadows is remembered as the first temporary headquarters of the United Nations from 1946, and the scene of the momentous UN General Assembly vote on Palestine on November 29, 1947.

And it was in Flushing Meadows that the UNSCOP Report was submitted to the United Nations. The Ad Hoc Committee on Palestine formed a sub-Committee to draw up a detailed plan for the future government of Palestine.

On 19 November, the sub-committee recommended setting up a Commission including representatives from Guatemala, Iceland, Norway, Poland and Uruguay.

But Britain refused to implement a policy that was not acceptable to both sides, so the UN Palestine Commission never got off the ground. Britain administered Palestine alone during the transitional period.

On 20 November, the British Government unilaterally announced that the Mandate for Palestine would end on 14 May 1948.

At 4pm on Saturday, 29 November 1947, the 128th Plenary Meeting of the United Nations was held in the General Assembly Hall at Flushing Meadows. The historic Partition Plan (Resolution 181) was put to the vote.

Initially, 30 countries had indicated that they were in favour: Australia, Belgium, Bolivia, Brazil, Byelorussia, Canada, Costa Rica, Czechoslovakia, Denmark, Dominican Republic, Ecuador, France, Guatemala, Iceland, Luxembourg, Netherlands, New Zealand, Nicaragua, Norway, Panama, Paraguay, Peru, Poland, Sweden, South Africa, Ukraine, United States, Soviet Union, Uruguay and Venezuela.

Then three countries switched to in favour: Haiti, Liberia and Philippines, making a total of 33 countries in favour – and passing the two thirds mark.

Voting against were: Afghanistan, Cuba, Egypt, Greece, India, Iran, Iraq, Lebanon, Pakistan, Saudi Arabia, Syria, Turkey and Yemen.

Ten countries abstained: Argentina, Chile, Republic of China, Colombia, El Salvador, Ethiopia, Honduras, Mexico, the United Kingdom and Yugoslavia.

One country, Thailand, was absent.

Reverend William Hull describes what happened in Jerusalem when news of the UN vote reached the city:

"In no place in the world did the decision mean more than in Jerusalem. For centuries of time Jews all over the world had taken their oath: 'If I forget thee, O Jerusalem...', and in Jerusalem were those who, inspired by the sacredness of this spot, had come to make their homes there in a life-time remembrance of their oath.

"The night of November 29 we slept, but we must have been among the very few in Jewish Jerusalem who did. Our sleep was soon disturbed. There was seven hours difference in time, and it was after midnight when the result of the crucial vote was heard over the air from New York. Sleep fled, the street was full of riotous sound, but a riot of joy. Trucks passed, full of young and old, singing, shouting, waving flags, blowing trumpets.

"Above all rang out the triumphant cry: Medinat Ha'yehudim! (A Jewish State!) All that night and the next day Jewish Jerusalem gave itself over to a time devoted entirely to rejoicing. Young people danced the hora in the streets, British police and soldiers forgot their anti-Semitism and joined the Jews in their rejoicing, dancing and waving the blue and white flag of Zion. No one who was among the Jews in Jerusalem on Sunday, November 30, 1947, will forget it as long as he lives... We, too, joined the rejoicing crowds, and tears quickly came to our eyes as we met friends and shared their joy with them."

On May 14, 1948, the day the British Mandate expired, David Ben Gurion addressed the Jewish People's Council gathered at the Tel Aviv Museum, and read out the text of Israel's Declaration of Independence.

ERETZ YISRAEL [Hebrew - the Land of Israel, Palestine] was the birthplace of the Jewish people.

Here their spiritual, religious and political identity was shaped.

Here they first attained to statehood, created cultural values of national and universal significance and gave to the world the eternal Book of Books.

After being forcibly exiled from their land, the people kept faith with it throughout their Dispersion and never ceased to pray and hope for their return to it and for the restoration in it of their political freedom.

Impelled by this historic and traditional attachment, Jews strove in every successive generation to re-establish themselves in their ancient homeland.

In recent decades they returned in their masses. Pioneers, *ma'pilim* [(Hebrew) - immigrants coming to Eretz-Israel in defiance of restrictive legislation] and defenders, they made deserts bloom, revived the Hebrew language, built villages and towns, and created a thriving community controlling its own economy and culture, loving peace but knowing how to defend itself, bringing the blessings of progress to all the country's inhabitants, and aspiring towards independent nationhood.

In the year 5657 (1897), at the summons of the spiritual father of the Jewish State, Theodore Herzl, the First Zionist Congress convened and proclaimed the right of the Jewish people to national rebirth in its own country.

This right was recognized in the Balfour Declaration of the 2nd November, 1917, and re-affirmed in the Mandate of the League of Nations which, in particular, gave international sanction to the historic connection between the Jewish people and Eretz-Israel and to the right of the Jewish people to rebuild its National Home.

The catastrophe which recently befell the Jewish people - the massacre of millions of Jews in Europe - was another clear demonstration of the urgency of solving the problem of its homelessness by re-establishing in Eretz-Israel the Jewish State, which would open the gates of the homeland wide to every Jew and confer upon the Jewish people the status of a fully privileged member of the comity of nations.

Survivors of the Nazi holocaust in Europe, as well as Jews from other parts of the world, continued to migrate to Eretz-Israel, undaunted by difficulties, restrictions and dangers, and never ceased to assert their right to a life of dignity, freedom and honest toil in their national homeland.

In WW2, the Jewish community of this country contributed its full share to the struggle of the freedom- and peace-loving nations against the forces of Nazi wickedness and, by the blood of its soldiers and its war effort, gained the right to be reckoned among the peoples who founded the United Nations.

On the 29th November, 1947, the United Nations General Assembly passed a resolution calling for the establishment of a Jewish State in Eretz-Israel; the General Assembly required the inhabitants of Eretz-Israel to take such steps as were necessary on their part for the implementation of that resolution.

This recognition by the United Nations of the right of the Jewish people to establish their State is irrevocable. This right is the natural right of the Jewish people to be masters of their own fate, like all other nations, in their own sovereign State.

Accordingly we, members of the People's Council, representatives of the Jewish community of Eretz-Israel and of the Zionist movement, are here assembled on the day of the termination of the British mandate over Eretz-Israel and, by virtue of our natural and historic right and on the strength of the resolution of the United Nations General Assembly, hereby declare the establishment of a Jewish state in Eretz-Israel, to be known as the State of Israel.

WE DECLARE that, with effect from the moment of the termination of the Mandate being tonight, the eve of Sabbath, the 6th Iyar, 5708 (15th May, 1948), until the establishment of the elected, regular authorities of the State in accordance with the Constitution which shall be adopted by the Elected Constituent Assembly not later than the 1st October 1948, the People's Council shall act as a Provisional Council of State, and its executive organ, the People's Administration, shall be the Provisional Government of the Jewish State, to be called "Israel".

THE STATE OF ISRAEL will be open for Jewish immigration and for the Ingathering of the Exiles; it will foster the development of the country for the benefit of all its inhabitants; it will be based on freedom, justice and peace as envisaged by the prophets of Israel; it will ensure complete equality of social and political rights to all its inhabitants irrespective of religion, race or sex; it will guarantee freedom of religion, conscience, language, education and culture; it will safeguard the Holy Places of all religions; and it will be faithful to the principles of the Charter of the United Nations.

THE STATE OF ISRAEL is prepared to cooperate with the agencies and representatives of the United Nations in implementing the resolution of the General Assembly of the 29th November, 1947, and will take steps to bring about the economic union of the whole of Eretz-Israel.

WE APPEAL to the United Nations to assist the Jewish people in the building-up of its State and to receive the State of Israel into the comity of nations.

WE APPEAL - in the very midst of the onslaught launched against us now for months - to the Arab inhabitants of the State of Israel to preserve peace and participate in the upbuilding of the State on the basis of full and equal citizenship and due representation in all its provisional and permanent institutions.

WE EXTEND our hand to all neighbouring states and their peoples in an offer of peace and good neighbourliness, and appeal to them to establish bonds of cooperation and mutual help with the sovereign Jewish people settled in its own land. The State of Israel is prepared to do its share in a common effort for the advancement of the entire Middle East.

WE APPEAL to the Jewish people throughout the Diaspora to rally round the Jews of Eretz-Israel in the tasks of immigration and upbuilding and to stand by them in the great struggle for the realization of the age-old dream - the redemption of Israel.

Placing our trust in the "Rock of Israel", we affix our signatures to this proclamation at this session of the Provisional Council of State, on the soil of the homeland, in the city of Tel-Aviv, on this Sabbath eve, the 5th day of Iyar, 5708 (14th May, 1948).

Here is how Reverend Hull described Ben-Gurion's pronouncement of independence:

"After two thousand years of longing, hoping, suffering, praying the State of Israel was born.

"Blessed art Thou, O Lord, our God, King of the Universe, for keeping us alive, preserving us and permitting us to attain this day. Amen, Amen.

"People wept unashamedly. It was a historic moment, unique in world history since the day Abraham was called by God from Ur of the Chaldees to leave his home and come to a land he knew not, there to build a nation through which all the world was to be blessed."

There is a fascinating postscript to the story of William Hull. In 1962, as he was coming to the end of more than a quarter of a century in Jerusalem, he received a most unusual request from the Ministry of Religious Affairs: would he agree to be spiritual advisor to a Christian prisoner on death row.

The prisoner was Adolf Eichmann, who had helped mastermind the Holocaust and had been captured in a secret operation by the Mossad in Argentina.

Hull was appointed as Eichmann's spiritual counselor.

Hull was friendly with Tzvi Terlo, Israel's Assistant Attorney General, who had done much of the work in preparing the material for the prosecution case against Eichmann. Terlo told Hull:

"In all the world, you are the one Christian clergyman or priest who helped the Haganah to create the State. Now, out of all the clergymen in the world, you are the one who is ministering to Eichmann. It is ironical. God is laughing at us."

Hull and his wife met Eichmann in his cell several times, and Hull later wrote a book about his experiences, *Struggle for a Soul*. Hull was present when Eichmann was hanged, and he stayed with the body as it was taken outside and cremated. As a final act, he escorted the ashes to Jaffa, boarded an Israeli naval craft and carried the ashes six miles out, past Israeli territorial waters and poured the ashes into the sea.

Hull returned to Canada in 1962, and died in 1992.

Postscript

Today, in a world determined to delegitimise the Jewish State, the need for Christians to support Israel and the Jewish people is greater than ever.

In a world where the term "Christian Zionist" has become a political weapon in the hands of many of Israel's enemies, it is important to tell the story of the Christians who helped make the State of Israel a reality.

I believe that the Jewish world is duty-bound to honour the Christian heroes like the clergymen and agriculturalists featured in this book, and the Christian soldiers featured in my previous book. As my friend Jerry Klinger says, "they did what no Jew could do."

I believe that the State of Israel should also do more to formally acknowledge the contribution of these Christian heroes.

The mindset of these Christian heroes can be summed up in the words of Professor Lowdermilk, whose passionate scientific argument for the viability of a Jewish state in the decade following the 1939 White Paper was a rallying cry for Zionists:

"The movement for establishing a Jewish national home in Palestine is one of the most remarkable records of a people's struggle for national survival and self-expression."

6 Officers, 2 Lions, and 750 Mules
by Yanky Fachler

Between 1915 and 1940, six men spearheaded the re-emergence of a Jewish military ethos after 2,000 years. All six were British Zionist army officers. All six believed that Jews had to organize themselves into a coherent and proactive military force. All six fought the anti-Semitism of the British army authorities. Three officers were Jews. Three were Christians.

What a rattling good yarn. This fascinating book is an inspiring read for anyone who wants deeper insight into the origins of the State of Israel. **Howard Graham**

The book - what a title - is tremendous. The author's style is readable, and so much of the facts and profiles are really informative. **Gerald Gotzen**

Chutzpah
Unlocking the Maverick Mindset for Success
by Yanky Fachler

Richard Branson, Donald Trump, Steven Spielberg, Oprah Winfrey and James Dyson have it in huge quantities. In Latin America, it's called "cojones". Dictionaries define it as "shameless audacity". But we all know it by the wonderfully evocative Yiddish term - "chutzpah". Yanky claims that chutzpah is a gene in our DNA that we can all tap into.

Most people don't succeed because they don't have the guts to take action. They need chutzpah. They can get inspired to be courageous in the new book Chutzpah. *It's actually fantastic.* **Dr. Joe Vitale, Hypnotic Marketing, Inc., USA**

Your Chutzpah book is awesome! **David Frey, Marketing Best Practices, USA**

157

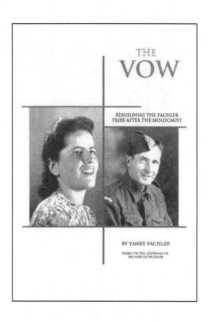

The Vow
Rebuilding the Fachler Tribe after the Holocaust
by Yanky Fachler

This is the true story of Eva and Eli Fachler, who arrived in Britain from Nazi Germany as teenage refugees in the months before the outbreak of WW2. The book traces their childhood growing up in Frankfurt and Berlin respectively, their escape by train to Britain via Holland, their experiences in wartime Britain, and the vow they made under the wedding canopy in December 1944 to rebuild the family that had been decimated in the Holocaust.

About the author

Yanky is a writer, broadcaster, trainer and motivational speaker. He is the media spokesperson for Ireland's Jewish Representative Council, and founder member of Ireland's Holocaust Memorial Day Committee.

He writes and speaks extensively on business topics and on Jewish history.

His books include *The Vow: rebuilding the Fachler family after the Holocaust; 6 Officers, 2 Lions and 750 Mules* – the story of 6 British army officers who helped create a Jewish military ethos after 2,000 years; *Chutzpah: Unlocking the maverick mindset;* and a chapter called *Ireland, Israel, and the challenge of innovation and enterprise* in *What did we do right? Global perspectives on Ireland's 'Miracle.'*

Partial list of Yanky's history talks:

Lt Col John Henry Patterson and Captain Jug 'O Whiskey (Jabotinsky)

God's Little Errand Boys

Monsignor Hugh O'Flaherty – the Vatican Pimpernel

The Dreyfus Case

A second-generation Jew revisits Poland

Mead and Lowdermilk – two influential agriculturists

The Kindertransports

The Jewish Brigade

The Zion Mule Corps and the Jewish Legion

Rev John Grauel and the Exodus

Key documents in modern Zionist history

To order books, or to book Yanky as a speaker, please contact yanky@eircom.net, +353 86 8575162

Printed and bound in Ireland by

The Book Producers Ltd.
www.thebookproducers.ie